Lord and Pharaoh

If this chapter be recited for the deceased he shall be strong upon earth before Ra, and he shall have a comfortable burial [or tomb] before Osiris, and it shall be of great benefit to a man in the Underworld. Sepulchral bread shall be given unto him, and he shall come forth into the presence [of Ra] day by day, and every day, regularly, and continually.

Book of Coming Forth by Day [The Book of the Dead, ca. 1550 B.C.][1]

In Egyptology, as in everything else, the great idea is to do something new and sensational and not laboriously potter over what has been done before.

William Randolph Hearst, 1900[2]

Lord and Pharaoh

Carnarvon and the Search for **Tutankhamun**

Brian Fagan

Left Coast Press Inc.

Walnut Creek, California

LEFT COAST PRESS, INC.
1630 North Main Street, #400
Walnut Creek, CA 94596
www.LCoastPress.com

Left Coast Press Inc.

ISBN.978-1-62958-151-4 paperback
ISBN 978-1-62958-152-1 Institutional eBook
ISBN 978-1-62958-153-8 consumer eBook

Library of Congress Cataloging-in-Publication Data
Fagan, Brian M., author.
 Lord and Pharaoh : Carnarvon and the search for Tutankhamun / Brian Fagan.
  pages cm
 Includes bibliographical references and index.
  ISBN 978-1-62958-151-4 (pbk. : alk. paper)—ISBN 978-1-62958-152-1 (institutional ebook)—ISBN 978-1-62958-153-8 (consumer ebook)
 1. Tutankhamen, King of Egypt. 2. Tutankhamen, King of Egypt—Tomb. 3. Carnarvon, George Edward Stanhope Molyneux Herbert, Earl of, 1866–1923. 4. Excavations (Archaeology)—Egypt—Valley of the Kings. 5. Valley of the Kings (Egypt)—Antiquities. 6. Egyptologists—Great Britain—Biography. I. Title.
 DT87.5.F34 2015
 932.014—dc23

                    2014046725

∞™ Printed in the United States of America
The paper used in this publication meets the minimum requirements of American National Standard for Information Sciences—Permanence of Paper for Printed Library Materials, ANSI/NISO Z39.48–1992.

Contents

List of Illustrations

Preface

I wrote this book because I wanted to know more about Lord Carnarvon, the aristocratic half of the famous Carnarvon-Carter partnership that discovered Tutankhamun's tomb in 1922. The Fifth Earl is a little-known figure in the drama compared with his archaeological colleague, Howard Carter, who has been the subject of several admirable biographies. But it was the Earl who gambled large sums on finding Tutankhamun—and won. Unfortunately, much of Carnarvon's correspondence was destroyed by World War II bombs, so to write a comprehensive life would be a time-consuming, difficult task. I thought, however, that a short essay would be a viable alternative that would satisfy my curiosity, and so it has proved.

As I moved the story into the Valley of the Kings, I was startled to find that almost nothing has been published about the young pharaoh himself beyond his tomb, much speculation, and some bare details of his short reign. What was he like as a person? Did he really restore ancient religious beliefs? Who reigned on his behalf? Bookshelves of popular and more technical works discuss the discovery, but Tutankhamun himself and his life have escaped much scrutiny beyond the basics.[*] Clearly, there was a fascinating story here, too. So I decided to do something unconventional and write a parallel account of both men. They turned out to have much in common—privileged upbringings, frail health, isolation from the real world, ingrained senses of entitlement, and even a common cause of death—from the effects of an infected mosquito bite. And, of course, they "met" in the end with the discovery of the pharaoh's tomb. The result is a complex but fascinating story that opens windows into the long-forgotten reign of a boy king and the volatile Egyptological world of a century ago with its rich, often competing, personalities. I thoroughly enjoyed my excursion into two unusual lives.

The book is a straightforward narrative, insofar that it is possible to achieve this with two separate lives over three thousand years apart. The first two chapters set the stage and bring the story of the Valley of the Kings up to the moment in 1914 when American digger Theodore Davis announced (wrongly) that the Valley was exhausted, that no more tombs awaited discovery. We then embark on the two biographies, starting with Tutankhamun's early life. The chapters that follow alternate between the pharaoh and the Earl as they pass through different stages of their lives. Obviously, in the case of Tutankhamun, there are major gaps in the story that will never be known. I have used some of the artifacts from his tomb, including personal possessions, to fill out the portrait. I've also made use of limited amounts of fictional dialogue where I

[*]Charlotte Booth's *The Boy Behind the Mask: Meeting the Real Tutankhamun* (Oxford: Oneworld Publications, 2007) is an exception.

feel it helps the momentum of the story—but dialogue that must have approximated to what was really said at the time. With Tutankhamun's death and its aftermath, the narrative shifts to the search for, and discovery of, the tomb, when Carnarvon's gamble pays off. The story ends with the opening of the burial chamber, Carnarvon's death, and the troubled aftermath. Egyptologists continue to argue, sometimes passionately, over such controversies as the cause of the pharaoh's death, or whether his widow wrote to the Hittites. In most cases, I've discussed these arguments briefly in the Notes, to avoid interrupting the narrative.

This book is a microcosm of archaeological discovery, but it's also an account of a changing Egyptological scene. When Carnarvon arrived, wealthy benefactors employed archaeologists and shared in the finds. Then Tutankhamun came along at a time of rising Egyptian nationalism, and the archaeological world changed, too. Institutions replaced individuals; wealthy patricians no longer received ancient treasures.

The closing chapter is something completely different—an essay aimed at archaeologists about writing a book like this.

Let the play begin . . . "Life! Prosperity! Health!"

Acknowledgments

This book has benefited from advice from many Egyptologists over the years, some, alas, deceased. I am grateful to them all, too many to list. Aiden Dodson advised me at critical points. My esteemed colleague Stuart Smith read the entire manuscript and corrected my sins, for which I will be eternally grateful. Nadia Durrani encouraged me at key moments. My literary guru, Shelly Lowenkopf, was always there for me, especially at the "eureka" moment when the idea of a parallel biography came to mind. He also advised me on dialogue. Steve Brown drew the plans and maps with his usual skill. Detta Penna, Stacey Sawyer, and Ryan Harris skillfully guided the manuscript through production and saved me from many errors. My greatest debt is to my good friend Mitch Allen, who agreed to publish *Lord and Pharaoh*. Our relationship goes back many years and encompasses several books, which I've enjoyed writing.

Author's Note

Geographical place names are spelled according to the most common usages. In the case of major locations, I have tended to use the modern or historical names. For example, Thebes is used as the name for ancient Luxor, the Waset of Ancient Egypt. I use the Levant (the Eastern Mediterranean coastal region), the Near East, and Southwest Asia interchangeably.

Ancient Egyptian spellings are a minefield for the nonspecialist, but, once again, I've used the most common renderings.

Ancient Egyptian chronologies are still uncertain and vary from publication to publication. There are high and low chronologies for the ancient Near East, which reflect radiocarbon dates (higher chronology) and more conservative timescales based on historical documents and events. Thus, the dates of reigns quoted here should be regarded as good-faith approximations.

The B.C./A.D. convention is used for dates.

Measurements are given in metric with equivalents in brackets.

The various tombs in the Valley of the Kings have long-established identification numbers habitually used by Egyptologists. For instance, Tutankhamun's tomb is KV 62. I identify these numbers on a sepulcher's first appearance in the text and on the map of the Valley.

To give a historical flavor to the book, I've relied heavily on Harry Burton's superb pictures of the tomb, which give a vivid impression of what Carnarvon and Carter faced.

Brian Fagan
February 2015

A Valley of Pharaohs

Horus, Mighty Bull, Beloved of Truth
He of the two ladies, Risen with the fiery serpent, Great of strength
Horus of gold, Perfect of years, He who makes hearts live
He of the sedge and bee Aakheperkara [Upper and Lower Egypt]
Son of Ra Thutmose living forever and eternity.[1]

Egyptian pharaohs, glorified by their imposing titles, presided over the longest-lived state of the ancient world, which endured for over three thousand years after the unification of Upper and Lower Egypt in about 3100 B.C. Centuries of precedents and rituals surrounded the divine ruler that was the pharaoh. He (and occasionally she) was the embodiment of the Egyptian state, beloved by the sun god Ra, and a person apart from mere mortals. His or her subjects approached the throne prostrating themselves seven times, then seven times more. The pharaohs were divine monarchs who assumed that their deaths were merely a step from their rule on earth to continued kingship in the realm of eternity. Their tombs were portals to the underworld, carved below the earth as a gateway to their glorious immortality alongside the sun god. Hundreds of artists and craftspeople labored over royal sepulchers, filling them with magnificent treasures and adorning the walls with exquisite reliefs and paintings that reflected an elaborate cosmology and religious philosophy. For five centuries after 1539 B.C., the pharaohs constructed their tombs in a remote, dusty valley known today as The Valley of the Kings.

The Valley of the Gate of the Kings

The rulers lay in an inconspicuous but magnificent burial ground that is now one of the most famous archaeological sites in the world. Its location has never been a mystery, for the Ancient Egyptians themselves ransacked the royal sepulchers in ancient

Lord and Pharaoh by Brian Fagan,
pp. 13–26. © 2015 Left Coast Press, Inc. All rights reserved.

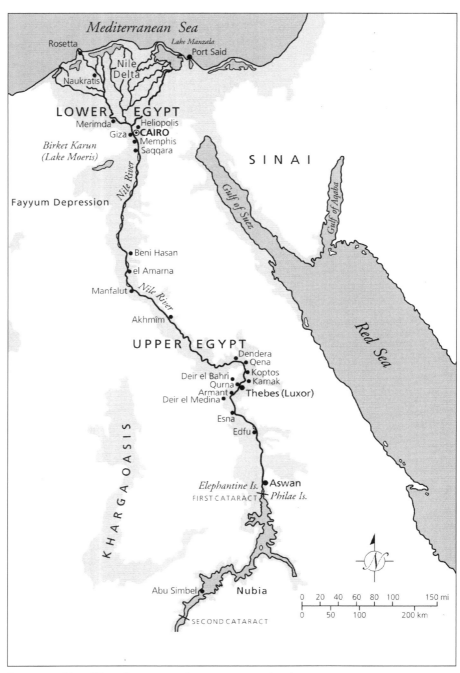

Figure 1.1   Map of Egypt showing major locations mentioned in the text.

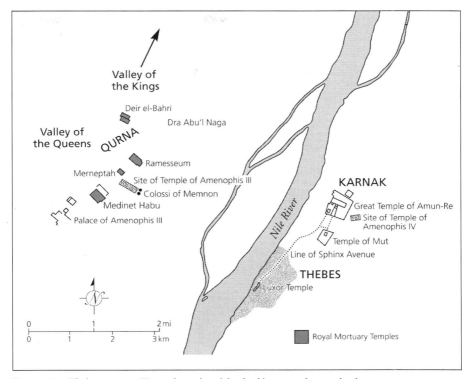

Figure 1.2   Thebes, ancient Waset, the realm of the dead being on the west bank.

times. The Greek geographer Strabo visited Upper Egypt in 25 B.C. and wrote of the west bank opposite what is now Luxor that "above the Memnonium [the mortuary temple of Ramesses II] are tombs of kings, which are stone-hewn, are about forty in number, are marvelously constructed, and are a spectacle worth seeing."[2] By Roman times, Egypt was a popular tourist destination. At least two thousand graffiti left by Greek and Latin visitors adorn ten Valley tombs with prominent entrances.

Wadi Biban el-Muluk ("The Valley of the Gates of the Kings") lies on the west bank of the Nile, opposite Waset (Thebes), now Luxor, "The Estate of Amun."[3] Here, the great temples of the creator god Amun at Karnak and Luxor were settings for public ceremonies and processions. Every year during the second month of the early summer flood, the Opet festival saw the boatlike shrine of Amun process from Karnak to Luxor, proclaiming that the king had renewed his ka, or spiritual essence, in the innermost shrine of Amun himself. The great temples were statements of raw imperial power, where the gods received food offerings and found shelter. Amun's temples owned cattle and mineral rights and maintained enormous grain stores. The wealth of the large temples and the authority of their gods were such that the great shrines were

15

Figure 1.3a   The Valley of the Kings in the early twentieth century. © *Griffith Institute, University of Oxford.*

a major factor in the economy—and a significant presence in the affairs of state. All the myths and rituals, as well as the imposing temples, were symbols of the continuity of proper rule, of *ma'at*, "rightness," a philosophical concept absolutely central to Egyptian thinking and pharaonic rule.

The Estate of Amun encompassed the western bank. A flat plain extended from the river opposite Thebes to rocky hills laced with shaded gullies, an area associated by the Egyptians with the setting sun and the afterlife. The god's estate was a symbolic way of extending the notion of continuity into the realm of the dead in the west. Here the pharaohs created an elaborate necropolis, a city of the dead, where mummified, or at least bandaged, commoner and noble alike lay in a confusion of mortuary temples and sepulchers. Common folk lay in narrow clefts and defiles in the rocky hills, with perhaps an amulet or two in their wrappings. The elite in their multiroomed sepulchers could afford elaborate sarcophagi and all the panoply of mummification to ensure immortality in the Underworld. The pharaohs embraced eternity with elaborate mortuary temples among the sepulchers of commoners and nobles, all dedicated to Amun-Re and lay in splendidly furnished underground tombs, cut into the rock of the Wadi Biban el-Muluk.

Figure 1.3b The Valley of the Kings today. *From Markh from en.wikipedia.*

The mountains to the west of the great river were where the sun set, the realm of death. And it was in their shadow that the pharaohs constructed their underground sepulchers. Wadi Biban el-Muluk is a dry river valley of eroded slopes and small dry water courses. A pyramid-shaped peak dominates the much-eroded defile, sacred to the goddess Hathor, guardian of the cemeteries on the west bank of the Nile. The first pharaoh to be buried in the Valley was probably Tuthmosis I, in about 1518 B.C., who apparently decided to separate his mortuary temple from his burial place.[4] For the next five centuries, the pharaohs of the Eighteenth, Nineteenth, and Twentieth Dynasties (1539–1075 B.C.) built their rock-cut tombs in the Valley. The ravine was remote and easily guarded, but its symbolic position was all-important. The hills behind the west bank formed the horizon of the setting sun, the realm of death. The main, eastern branch of the Valley, known to the Egyptians as *te set aat* ("The Great Place") contains most of the royal sepulchers. The purpose was common to all, but the lavish decoration and rich furnishings reflected not only the exquisite craftsmanship of royal artisans but also the rich philosophical beliefs of an ever-changing civilization.

Geologically, Wadi Biban el-Muluk is a complex place, its topography much eroded by rare, intense rainstorms. The light brown rocks of the Valley are mainly limestone with underlying layers of shale, relatively soft formations that made it easier for tomb workers to carve rock-cut sepulchers deep into bedrock. To the pharaohs, death was merely a step in the transition from ruling on earth to being a king in the immortality of the underworld. Royal tombs were portals to this realm as well as nether regions themselves, places built totally underground according to long-established precedent. When not crowded with visitors, they can be mystical, even scary, places. Many years ago, when fewer people were around, I visited the Valley while lecturing on a package tour. We paused for a break, so I slipped away from everyone and went into the tomb of Ramesses III. The lights were on, so I walked rapidly into the depths of the sepulcher, knowing that time was short. As I reached the burial chamber, the lights went out. The utter darkness and stillness settled around me like a blanket. The effect was mesmerizing. I'm not exaggerating when I say that I could literally feel the presence of the pharaoh. Then the lights went on and the spell was broken. I had briefly glanced into the underworld of eternity.

For all its profound ritual ambiance, the Valley of the Kings was a vast underground treasure house, with riches beyond imagining there for the taking. Ruthless tomb robbers emptied many of the sepulchers within a few generations. Later came treasure hunters, tourists, and finally archaeologists, the latter in search of the ultimate Holy Grail—an undisturbed pharaoh's tomb.

Belzoni's Tomb

When the Romans departed, the Valley faded into oblivion, the tombs inhabited by a few Christian hermits.[5] Over the centuries, it remained a remote defile of scree-laden hillsides, dry gullies, and cliffs. It's hard to imagine the Valley as it was as recently as the 1920s. Today there are booths and coffee shops, paved roads, parking lots for coaches, and restrooms. Wadi Biban el-Muluk has become a popular tourist destination, jammed with package tours and confused visitors. You wait in lines to inspect those tombs that are open to the public.

Only the occasional traveler explored the royal burial ground until the nineteenth century, among them an Englishman, Richard Pococke, in 1730. He thought that he identified about eighteen tombs, only nine of which could be entered. In 1768, Scottish traveler James Bruce described frescoes of harpists in Ramesses III's tomb, which he illustrated with fanciful abandon. The Valley was a remote curiosity until Napoléon Bonaparte invaded Egypt in 1798, his idea being to secure a strategic passage to India across the Isthmus of Suez. He took with him 140 savants, under the leadership of Vivant Denan, charged with describing Egypt, ancient and modern. For three years, a diminishing number of scientists traveled the Nile alongside the 4,000-man army. Savant and soldier alike gasped in admiration at the temples of Luxor and Karnak, at a hitherto unknown civilization quite unlike those of Greece and Rome. Denan accompanied a military party to the Valley of the Kings. To his intense frustra-

Figure 1.4   Napoléon's savants examine the Sphinx at Giza (from *Description de l'Égypte*). *Vivant Denon,* *1830.*

tion, he was allowed a mere three hours to examine six tombs. While he returned to France with Napoléon in 1799, his fellow savants embarked on a survey of Egypt that was to appear in the multivolume *Description de l'Égypte*, one of the classics of Egyptology. The *Description* contained the first systematic map of the Valley, which recorded sixteen tombs and, in the western arm, the beautiful tomb of Amenophis III.

Napoléon's savants revealed the astounding glories of Ancient Egypt and set off an aggressive search for Egyptian antiquities, notably in the hands of the French and British consuls, the Piedmontese-born Colonel Bernardino Drovetti and Henry Salt, a more scholarly diplomat. Both saw it as part of their charge to collect antiquities and sell them to major European museums. The competition was intense. The two men laid claims to most of the Estate of Amun. Drovetti dug frantically accompanied by his gang of what might charitably be called ruffians. Salt employed one of the most remarkable figures to work in the Valley of the Kings—Giovanni Belzoni. He became Drovetti's deadly rival. Blows were exchanged, guns threatened. Both were quite capable of lying in wait for a competitor with a gun.

Padua-born Giovanni Battista Belzoni was an imposing figure, who stood well over 2 meters (6 feet). Women are said to have found his curly black hair and broken English accent irresistible. As a young man, he sold religious relics across Europe, then became a circus performer and strongman in London. The "Patagonian Sampson" be-

19

Figure 1.5 Giovanni Belzoni in Turkish costume. *From* Narrative of the Operations and Recent Discoveries Within the Pyramids, Temples, Tombs and Excavations in Egypt and Nubia *by Giovanni Battista Belzoni, London, 1820.*

came a minor celebrity, famous for his achievements of strength and stagecraft. Years of show business gave Belzoni an expertise with weights, levers, and gunpowder, which was to serve him well along the Nile. He came to Egypt in 1815, accompanied by his long-suffering Irish wife Sarah, looking for work mechanizing agriculture and failed abysmally. In desperation, he accepted an offer to collect antiquities for Henry Salt. Belzoni was the ideal person for the job. Quite apart from his engineering skills, he was adept at dealing with the local people. He also seems to have possessed a rare quality, an instinct for archaeological discovery. The professional tomb robbers of the village of Qurna in the Theban Necropolis took a liking to the tall strong man, who enjoyed meals with them, the food cooked with broken mummy cases as firewood. Belzoni followed them into narrow, mummy-packed defiles. Fortunately, he had no sense of smell, but he complained that "mummies were rather unpleasant to swallow."

Belzoni came to the Valley of the Kings in 1816, well aware that the Romans had said there were as many as forty-seven tombs in the Valley. Belzoni counted ten or eleven that he considered to be royal sepulchers and began by puttering around the western arm, where he soon found the tomb of the courtier turned pharaoh Ay, who was to play an important role in Tutankhamun's life (see Chapter 5). But the Paduan was after much more important prey—royal tombs. In August 1817, he returned to the western arm and soon concluded that there was nothing to find, and so he moved into the Valley of the Kings itself. In October, he set twenty men to work in small groups, working in different places. Four days later, he found the sepulcher of Prince Mentuherkhepeshef, Hereditary Prince, Royal Scribe, Son of Pharaoh, Beloved by Him, Chief Inspector of Troops.[6] The tomb (KV 19) is remarkable for its painted scenes of the young prince in the presence of the gods.

Then it rained, a rare occurrence in Thebes. Torrents of floodwater cascaded down a slope close to the emptied tomb of Ramesses I (KV 16), which Belzoni had found a short time earlier. Convinced there was another tomb nearby, Belzoni set his men to work. Two days later, a cutting in the rock appeared. Five-and-a half meters (18 feet) below the surface, a tomb entrance emerged from the rubble. Eventually, one of the smallest workers was able to crawl under the lintel. He emerged into two richly decorated corridors, a flight of stairs, and an open pit. Belzoni had discovered the most magnificent sepulcher in the Valley (KV 17), that of the pharaoh Seti I, father of Ramesses II, who had died around 1300 B.C.

As he crawled through the first rubble-strewn passage, Belzoni saw great vultures hovering above them. Down the stairway, the Sun God lurked in all his flamboyant manifestations. His solar boat journeyed through the fourth division of the underworld on the right. On the left it entered the fifth hour, drawn by gods and goddesses. Everything ended at the pit with a wall beyond, a sump for flood waters as well as a device to mislead tomb robbers. In that it failed, for there was a hole on the opposite side.

The next day, Belzoni returned with two stout beams to bridge the pit. He squeezed through the robber's hole and found himself in a pillared hall with magnificent figures of the pharaoh being embraced by deities and scenes of the underworld. A false chamber beyond adorned with deliberately unfinished figures aimed to deceive robbers, but failed to do so. Belzoni and his men tapped the walls and broke through to another corridor that led eventually to the burial chamber. The art on the walls entranced Belzoni with its mastery, but it was nothing compared with the six-pillared burial chamber with the deities and forces of the underworld, the Sun God's barque, and the now-divine pharaoh himself. But it was the sarcophagus that took Belzoni's breath away in the candlelight. The pharaoh had lain in a translucent alabaster sarcophagus. The lid was missing, but the entire coffin had been carved from a single block, carefully shaped for the king's body, even allowing for his folded headdress. The stone was from 5 to 10 centimeters (2 to 4 inches) thick, the sarcophagus itself over 2.75 meters (9 feet) long, carved with tiny figures inlaid in blue paste. At the bottom, the goddess Neith, slim and bare-breasted, waited to receive the king.

At the time, of course, Belzoni had no idea which pharaoh had lain in the tomb, for no one could read hieroglyphs. The mummy was missing. Except for some wooden figures, the sepulcher was empty. But it was a discovery of huge importance. People have argued endlessly as to whether Belzoni could be described as an archaeologist,

21

which by modern standards is certainly questionable. But no one denies that ultimately he was a showman looking for a profit. He saw the potential of the tomb immediately and made plans to copy the paintings for a replica of the tomb. With great difficulty, he managed to remove the sarcophagus from the burial chamber.

Giovanni Belzoni had discovered four royal tombs in the Valley in twelve days, but it was his last find that would make headlines. Over many months, he and artist Alessandro Ricci copied the paintings and made "squeezes" to form the centerpiece of an exhibit in London at which he would display his spectacular finds—for a shilling each. In March 1820, he returned to London. The celebrated publisher John Murray published Giovanni's account of his adventures at the end of the year. *Narrative of the Operations and Discoveries within the Pyramids, Temples, Tombs, and Excavations in Egypt and Nubia* is a hastily written compilation of journals and notes that is unpolished, often vague, yet has a pleasant immediacy. Murray introduced the Paduan to influential people. He found himself a celebrity—tall, good looking, and newly arrived from the East. At a time when many people were much shorter of stature, Belzoni awed those he met. Wrote the poet Walter Scott: "The great lion—great in every sense— . . . is said completely to have overawed the Arabs . . . by his great strength, height, and energy."[7] The book was well received by the intelligentsia. The *Quarterly Review*, long a supporter of Belzoni, remarked prophetically in a long article that the author was a pioneer of antiquarian researches: "He points out the road and makes it easy for others to travel over." The comment was discerning. Belzoni literally put the Valley of the Kings on the archaeological map with his travelogue and with his imposing exhibition.

By lucky chance, he was able to rent the Egyptian Hall in Piccadilly in the heart of fashionable London, a building with an Egyptian façade recalling a temple pylon that stood out from its more sedate neighbors. Belzoni obtained the hall for the summer of 1821. Seti's tomb formed the centerpiece, a replica that focused on two chambers, the original rock-cut sepulcher being 100 meters (328 feet) long. These he set up at full size, using his copies, together with a small-scale model of the tomb and spectacular artifacts from his excavations. The exhibition opened to rapturous acclaim on May 1, 1821, proclaimed by no less than *The Times* to be a "multitude of collateral curiosities." Visitors passed between twelve underworld gods carrying a snake with human heads projecting from it to reach a chamber where the god Osiris welcomed the dead pharaoh, introduced by Horus. Ricci's drawings, at a sixth full size, lined the upstairs walls, so one could follow the sequence of chambers and decoration from one end to the other. Before the exhibit opened, with brilliant opportunism Belzoni unwrapped a mummy that was to appear in the exhibition for a group of professional men.

The alabaster sarcophagus did not appear in the show. Salt, who technically owned it, was anxious to sell it to the British Museum. Controversy surrounded the potential sale; Belzoni insisted he had a claim as the discoverer. The issue was unresolved when he embarked on a fatal expedition to West Africa in search of the source of the Niger River. In the end, in May 1824, Sir John Soane, a prominent architect and art collector, purchased the sarcophagus from Henry Salt for two thousand pounds. Giovanni and Sarah Belzoni received not a penny. The sarcophagus lies in the basement of Sir John's house, which is now a museum, where you can see it. But you will not have the pleasure of seeing a candle shine through the translucent sides, as was the case when Sir John opened his house for a distinguished audience to enjoy it.

Decipherment and Afterward

Belzoni had used battering rams, weights and levers, even gunpowder, along the Nile. His was a rollicking adventure, which he clearly enjoyed while seeking fame and fortune. But it was Seti's tomb that put him and the Valley in the limelight. Throughout his years in Egypt, Belzoni and his contemporaries were unable to read hieroglyphs, so the ownership of the tombs he discovered remained a mystery. The turning point came after years of sporadic work on the inscriptions on the trilingual Rosetta Stone, discovered by Napoleon's troops at the Nile Delta town of that name (*Rashid*, or Rosetta) in 1799. Thomas Young, an English doctor with broad research talents, identified some of the hieroglyphs as phonetic, but it was a young Frenchman and linguistic genius, Jean François Champollion (1790–1832), who unraveled the complex phonetic principles of hieroglyphs using pharaonic cartouches (ruler's names enclosed in ovals in inscriptions from the Abu Simbel temple and elsewhere) in September 1822. At the time, he was living in poverty in Paris. He is said to have rushed out of his room, shouting "I've got it" before collapsing in a dead faint.[8]

Full decipherment took at least a decade of close argument and painstaking research. Champollion made a triumphant visit to the Nile in 1828. For the first time, he and his companions could read temple and tomb inscriptions. They admired temples by moonlight and deciphered inscriptions on the go before spending four months in the Valley of the Kings, where they recorded the paintings and inscriptions of the sixteen accessible royal tombs, including Belzoni's sepulcher, subsequently identified as that of the great pharaoh Seti I, who reigned from 1291–1278 B.C. and was one of Egypt's most successful conquerors.

Until now Ancient Egypt had been little more than a moneymaking enterprise for a motley crowd of adventurers and treasure hunters. Fortunately, a few visitors came to the Nile in search of knowledge rather than artifacts. Just before Belzoni's exhibit opened in London, a young English artist, John Gardner Wilkinson (1797–1875), arrived in Cairo and threw himself into Egyptology.[9] For twelve years, he traveled along the river copying and deciphering inscriptions with meticulous care. He settled in the Theban Necropolis on the west bank, took up residence in a noble's tomb, which he furnished comfortably, and entertained visitors. Like everyone else, he used mummy cases as firewood, which emitted a horrible smell. Wilkinson lived well. One visitor wrote appreciatively of the "congenial perfume of savory viands." During his long stay, the artist surveyed and numbered the known tombs in the Valley, but his main interest was the tombs of the nobility, which yielded naturalistic scenes of daily life. After leaving Egypt in 1833, Wilkinson published *Manners and Customs of the Ancient Egyptians* (1837), a three-volume work that became a classic account of Ancient Egyptian civilization. He covered every aspect of Egyptian life from feasts to death, bringing a hitherto virtually unknown people into sharp focus, through inscriptions, paintings, papyri, and sites. He also established the first (inaccurate) chronology of the pharaohs, as well as writing a *Handbook for Travellers in Egypt* (1847), which accompanied generations of tourists to the Nile.

John Gardner Wilkinson made some of the first truly accurate copies of art from the Valley of the Kings and elsewhere, far superior to Champollion's work. As he left the Land of the Pharaohs, the days of the amateur treasure hunter were numbered, replaced by professionals, often representing museums in Europe. The German Karl Lepsius of the University of Berlin spent 1842–1845 in Egypt. He returned with copious records and 15,000 artifacts, including a column carefully dynamited from Seti's tomb.

Over the years that followed, serious research became more firmly entrenched, although there was still an epidemic of looting and dishonest acquisition. The French archaeologist Auguste Mariette(1821–1881) did much to stem looting by digging ahead of robbers, during a new era when the steamship and the railroad triggered a tourist boom that made Egypt much more accessible to the outside world. The Nile became a fashionable winter destination for the well-heeled and a stop-off point for British officials on their way to and from India. The tourist traveled upstream by railroad, steamer, or in a *dahabiyyah*, a vessel with a huge sail, which carried the boat upstream. It returned with the current or being towed by the crew. Such a trip took two months or so and was ideal for those of an artistic inclination.

With the assumption of British and French control over Egypt in 1881, the British Consul General, Sir Evelyn Baring, later Lord Cromer, and Gaston Maspero, the French Director General of Antiquities, built up the Antiquities Department into a more viable organization with inspectors who regulated all excavations along the Nile with a system of permits. Illegal excavation and looting faded into the background but still continued, because the potential rewards were enormous.

Cache of Pharaohs

The human urge to collect, to possess, has always been powerful, but no more so than in the case of tourists who visited Luxor after the 1860s. As steamship traffic increased, so did the supply of mummies and antiquities large and small, which seemed inexhaustible. The professional tomb robbers of Qurna, befriended by Giovanni Belzoni a half century earlier, prospered comfortably off winter visitors. Two thieves, Ahmed Abd el-Rasul and his brother Mohammed, were especially successful. By chance, Ahmed, while looking for a goat, had come across an exceptionally rich cache of royal mummies and burial furniture stashed in an abandoned hillside shaft. He and his brother mined the cache for small numbers of superb antiquities, which they smuggled into Luxor hidden among bundles of clothing or vegetables for the bazaar. Wary, with good reason, of the authorities, they sold only a few prize items at a time, mostly exquisite canopic jars, jewelry, and *ubshabtis*, mostly from high priests and royal relatives of the XXI Dynasty, to avoid deflating the market.[10]

Inevitably, American and English tourists boasted of their purchases. Word reached Gaston Maspero, who suspected that an important find had been made. Some of the Rasuls' pieces could have only royal associations. He sent one of his staff in the guise of a wealthy tourist with money to spend, who bought a few choice pieces from the two men. When a dealer brought him a magnificent funerary statuette that could have come only from a XXI Dynasty tomb, the agent finally met Ahmed Abd el-Rasul and Mustapha Aga Ayat, a Turk who was consular agent for Belgium, Britain, and Russia in Luxor. The post gave him diplomatic immunity and superb cover for dealing in antiquities, most of which came from the Rasuls.

The brothers were arrested and tortured, but they feverishly denied their guilt. They were released for lack of witnesses. But a family quarrel now erupted over the sharing of the loot, and the Antiquities Service renewed its inquiries. Mohammed soon realized that his only salvation was to confess everything and obtain immunity from punishment. A few days later, he led a small party to the site of the cache, including Émile Brugsch, a trusted member of the Antiquities Department staff, Maspero being out of the country. Armed to the teeth, Brugsch was lowered into the deep shaft with a supply of candles. He had been led to believe that the find was that of a wealthy official's tomb. What he saw in the candlelight was "a whole vault of pharaohs. And what Pharaohs! Perhaps the most illustrious in the history of Egypt, Thutmose III and Seti I, Ahmose the Liberator and Ramses the Conqueror."[11] He wondered if he was dreaming. Coffins of famous queens lay in confusion, alongside bronze libation jars and other priceless objects.

Recent research has shown that the royal mummies in the cache were moved several times, robbed of their jewelry, and then rebandaged before being dumped in cheap coffins in the Deir el-Bahri cleft. One can imagine the desperate necropolis guards working in the dead of night, spiriting away royal mummies and their grave offerings one step ahead of looters, then hiding them in a remote defile, where they escaped discovery until the Rasuls came along.

Brugsch soon recovered from his astonishment, hired 300 workmen, emptied the shaft in short order, and transported the precious contents to the Nile. The government steamer *el-Menshieh* carried a load of about fifty pharaohs, queens, and nobles, also some 5,900 antiquities, downstream to Cairo. Maspero recorded the scenes of lamentation as the precious cargo left Thebes, women wailing, men firing their rifles in the air. Cynical observers wondered if they were bewailing the loss of a lucrative source of income.

In the Cairo Museum, Maspero and his colleagues unwrapped some of the royal mummies and gazed on the features of some of Egypt's most famous rulers. Seti I was

Figure 1.6 Pharaoh Seti I. *From* Catalogue General Antiquites Egyptiennes du Musee du Caire: The Royal Mummies. *Le Caire : Imprimerie de L'institut Francais D'archeologie Orientale, 1912 Catalogue General Antiquites Egyptiennes du Musee du Caire DT57.C2 vol 59*

the best preserved: "A calm and gentle smile still played over his mouth." He was the epitome of a powerful, competent ruler, in his day the most powerful monarch on earth. Belzoni would have been fascinated and pleased that the owner of the most spectacular tomb in the Valley of the Kings had survived for posterity. The cache itself had a complex history, jammed as it was into the tomb of a high priest named Pinudjem II. The guards left the mummies of his family undisturbed and crammed the pharaohs and others into the corridors and side chambers of the tomb.

In the years that followed, there were other discoveries, notably sixteen tombs added to the Valley inventory by the French archaeologist Victor Loret. He uncovered a second royal cache in the Tomb of the pharaoh Amenhotep II, where he located coffins and mummies of nine pharaohs, among them Ramesses II himself and some later kings. The search for royal tombs continued unabated, with permits to excavate in the Valley of the Kings being the most eagerly sought after of all, reserved by Maspero for the wealthy and well connected. Among them was Theodore Davis, an American lawyer and millionaire robber baron, who first came as a tourist, then acquired the concession for the Valley of the Kings. Few pharaohs escaped his hard-driving excavations, but one of them was a little known ruler—Tutankhamun.

Chapter 2

Discoveries of a Self-Made Man

"We are very happy on this wonderful Nile," wrote Theodore Davis in 1894.[1] He and his devoted mistress, Emma Andrews, progressed upstream, as they did every winter, in a *dahabiyyah*, with "a new and very good grand piano." By this time, they were very familiar with the land of the pharaohs. Davis had first visited Egypt in 1887 on the advice of friends. He liked it so much that he returned two years later, when he rented his first *dahabiyyah*. By this time, his doctors had advised him to spend the winters in a warm climate, so he spent half of each year in Europe or Egypt. He could afford to. At the age of thirty-nine he had acquired wealth beyond his wildest dreams.

A Self-Made Man

Theodore Davis (1837–1915) was a farmer's son from Michigan who left home at age fifteen, became a land inspector for a Great Lakes canal company, and traveled west and apprenticed himself to a lawyer just as the railroad reached Iowa City in 1855. A self-taught attorney, he prospered, a wiry, muscular man with a strong jaw and a high forehead, known for his stylish clothes. During the Civil War, he invested judiciously in real estate and became quite wealthy, moving to New York City in 1865 just as the post-Civil War boom began. Hard working and determined, but unhappily married, Davis became involved in insolvent national banks at a time when corruption and underhand dealing were routine. He made a fortune of at least three million dollars as a discreet, efficient, if not entirely scrupulous, attorney, specializing in banks and canals. By 1877, he had secured his fortune by expert, and shady, dealings involving the insolvent Ocean Bank in New York and the Lake Superior Ship Canal, Railway, and Iron Company. Despite prolonged legal maneuvers, Theodore Davis had achieved a level of wealth and power that enabled him to travel widely and to live in high style. He built an opulent mansion in Newport, Rhode Island. Now semiretired, but still actively involved in mining and railroad construction in the West, he remained an aggressive, active man with an ability to focus single-mindedly on whatever interested him. Despite constant legal challenges, even Congressional inquiries, he now spent the winters in Europe or Egypt with Emma, traveling in high style and luxury.

During his initial travels, Davis's passion was fine art, a common pastime for robber barons of the day anxious for social standing and obsessed with display. His competitive side and the excitement of the chase led him to buy not only Old Masters but also the works of modern artists such as Monet. Like other very wealthy buyers, he relied on expert advice, much of it from a Lithuanian-American named Bernhard Berenson, who was to become one of the great art scholars of the twentieth century. Berenson's wife Mary described Davis as "a man of power and character, who observed a great deal."[2] It was he who, some years later, persuaded Davis to purchase a Leonard da Vinci that turned out to be a forgery. He shrugged off the loss as part of the game.

Davis's first trips up the Nile were purely social. He traveled, like so many affluent tourists, from hotel to hotel, or just sailing along the river. He collected a few antiquities in Luxor and paid his first visit to the Valley of the Kings at the height of the winter season, on February 2, 1890. Emma in particular was appalled by the destruction on every side, with the government apparently doing nothing to prevent unlawful excavation. In late 1892, he again rented a *dahabiyyah*, sailing this time with both his wife Annie and Emma. By now, he was reading seriously about Egyptology, notably Flinders Petrie's widely read *Ten Years Digging in Egypt*, also works by the French antiquities official Auguste Mariette and Wallis Budge, a British Museum official notorious for his underhand dealings.[3] The months along the river were so seductive that at the end of the trip, he commissioned his own luxurious *dahabiyyah*, the *Beduin*, complete with carpets and "spring beds." It was 24 meters (80 feet) long, one of the fastest on the river. Year after year, Davis and Emma Andrews followed the same routine. They wined and dined archaeologists wherever they stopped and visited all the major sites.

People like Davis, immeasurably wealthy, experienced travelers, and socially connected, were the cream of the Egyptian tourist crop. Few built their own *dahabiyyahs*, even fewer developed a strong enough interest in Egyptology to sponsor excavations. Inevitably those with even a mild enthusiasm for the subject, or a desire to collect some choice antiquities, came in contact with archaeologists, who had relationships with both dealers and officials. Someone like Davis, a regular winter visitor, eventually met virtually everyone working on the major sites, especially the professional artists and excavators, also government officials. In those days, with no government grants, any serious digging required sponsors, as well as permits from the Antiquities Department. So the wealthy found themselves discreetly sought after for excavation funds, which, in Davis's case, for an entire season were a fraction of what he would routinely pay for a painting in Italy on his way home.

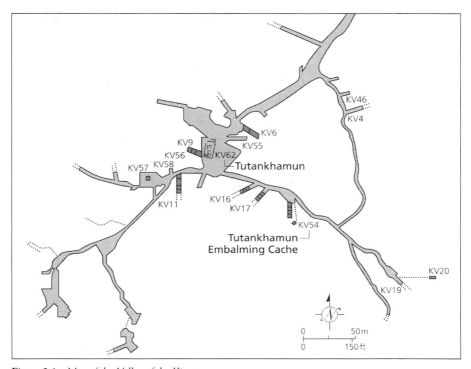

Figure 2.1 Map of the Valley of the Kings.

Theodore Davis entertained two British Egyptologists, Percy Newberry and his protégé Howard Carter, to dinner in 1901. Both were accomplished artists and archaeologists, who had long experience of copying tomb paintings. Howard Carter (1874–1939) was of lowly origin, a major handicap in class-conscious Britain, but his extraordinary artistic talents and a period working with Flinders Petrie, an expert excavator by the standards of the day, gave him exceptional credentials for a self-taught archaeologist.[4] Despite being strong-minded, obstinate, and conscious of his social inferiority, Carter was a remarkably gifted excavator with an encyclopedic knowledge of the Valley of the Kings and Upper Egypt's rich sites. In 1899, Gaston Maspero had appointed him Inspector of Antiquities for Upper Egypt, a job that included responsibility for the Valley of the Kings.

Carter and Davis became friends, perhaps because they both came from humble backgrounds and also spoke their minds, something somewhat alien to many Englishmen of the day. He entertained Davis, allowed him to attend the opening of a mummy, and showed him tombs that were closed to the public. They spoke frankly to each other, a big attraction for Davis, who liked straightforward people. He suggested that his visitor might be interested in sponsoring excavations in the Valley, to which the American agreed at once. Such an arrangement on a long-term basis would give him something interesting to do during his winter visits. From Carter's perspective, the funds enabled him to search for tombs, as well as carry out critically needed maintenance to prevent further damage from floods and visitors.

In January 1902, Gaston Maspero and Carter met with Davis and reached a long-term agreement for him to dig in the Valley. Davis would pay for excavations, but, unusual for the day, Egypt would retain all his finds, except for some duplicates. Carter recommended that he start work on either side of the narrow access road to the Valley, which needed to be widened to accommodate jostling crowds of tourists. Davis willingly agreed with Carter's recommendations. He always deferred to the professional archaeologists he retained, unlike other wealthy permit holders, who thought they knew best. The shift in responsibility to trained professionals was a watershed in Valley excavations, for which Theodore Davis should be given full credit. He was content to socialize and visit. He left the detail to those he hired at good salaries to do the work. A higher level of professionalism led to major discoveries almost immediately.

Tuthmosis and Hatshepsut

In 1903, Carter searched for the tomb of Tuthmosis IV, sensing he had been near it during the previous season. He found ritual objects bearing the name of the pharaoh, then the stairway and entrance. Inside, a steep, painted corridor and stairways led to the pillared, austerely decorated burial chamber. The carved granite sarcophagus was empty—the king's mummy had turned up in a cache in another tomb in 1898. It took ten days to clear the tomb, which yielded a jumble of magnificent objects, including a fragment of a colorful embroidered robe bearing the name of Tuthmosis's father, Amenhotep II.

This was Davis's first royal tomb, celebrated by the formal unwrapping of Tuthmosis IV's mummy in the Cairo Museum. Emma remarked that the pharaoh had "a fine, agreeable, well-preserved face." His was the first mummy to be X-rayed, transported to a private nursing home in a carriage for the purpose, the procedure in the hands of a well-known anatomist, Professor Elliot Grafton Smith.[5]

Carter had found hints that the sepulcher of Queen Hatshepsut, Egypt's first female pharaoh, lay nearby. He began the search in October 1903, working to clear a completely blocked tomb (KV 20) that had been known since Napoleon's time. The excavation was a miserable experience, the passages chock full of rubble, carved into unstable rock that could collapse at any moment. Conditions got worse and worse as Carter dug his way deeper, making his laborious way through fine bat dung that choked the workers' noses. The intense heat melted candles, so Davis brought in electric lights and an air pump. By January 1904, the excavation was over 150 meters (500 feet) below the surface. While Davis spent his time entertaining visitors aboard the *Beduin*, Carter labored far underground for another month. He reached a sealed doorway, then a chamber filled with rubble to the ceiling. By now conditions were hazardous. Carter emerged from the excavation dripping with sweat, covered in black dust. He had to lie down to recover from the effects of the foul air. Three weeks later, the chamber was cleared. Two empty sarcophagi and a red sandstone chest bearing Hatshepsut's name that once held the queen's viscera, lay inside. Fifteen limestone blocks lying on the floor had once adorned the walls, each inscribed with the *Amduat*, the ancient funerary text, "that which is in the Afterworld." More than 200 meters (700 feet) long, Hatshepsut's tomb was the deepest and largest in the Valley, but roughly executed. It was shared both by the Queen and her father Tuthmosis I, who had started the sepulcher. Carter described this excavation as the worst he had ever undertaken. Meanwhile, Davis, while giving credit to his archaeologist, basked in the acclaim. Hatshepsut's sarcophagus now adorns the Metropolitan Museum in New York.

Yuya and Tuya

Carter and Davis had worked well together, but change was afoot. Maspero shuffled his staff and transferred his inspector to Lower Egypt. Carter protested, but to no avail. He swapped places with another English archaeologist, James Quibell. An Oxford University graduate, Quibell had also learned archaeology under Flinders Petrie. He

Figure 2.2 Theodore Davis and colleagues, 1907. Left to right, Arthur and Hortense Weigall, Theodore Davis, and Edward Ayrton.

31

was well known for his discovery of the celebrated Narmer Palette at Hierakonopolis, upstream of Luxor, which commemorates the unification of Egypt in about 3100 B.C. He did not stay long, for Maspero decided to move him north again to supervise the ancient cemetery at Saqqara. While awaiting the transfer, Davis decided to move ahead anyway. He personally selected a narrow gully covered with granite chippings from the tombs of Ramesses III (KV 11) and XI (KV 4). Despite Quibell's objections, Davis told him to proceed with the clearance. From here onward, it was Davis who took charge of the excavations and decided where his archaeologist, and his workers, would dig. His objective was simple—clear the Valley completely and systematically until he knew it was devoid of more tombs. A huge slope of chippings 37 meters (120 feet) long and 9 meters (30 feet) high confronted Quibbell. The workers moved slowly to guard against cave-ins, examining every fragment for inscriptions or drawings. After three weeks of hard labor, to everyone except Davis's surprise, a tomb doorway emerged from the rubble (KV 46).

By this time, the new inspector had arrived, another young Englishman, Arthur Weigall, who was to become a player in the Tutankhamun saga.[6] The son of an army officer, he had worked with Petrie and had experience copying inscriptions. Davis had met him in Cairo and found him congenial. His arrival coincided with the exposure of the newly found doorway. He took over from the now-departed Quibbell and witnessed a spectacular discovery. Beyond the doorway was a sloping passage, then more steps that led to another door and to the burial chamber. Weigall and American artist Joseph Lindon Smith were first in and emerged breathless with excitement. Smith exclaimed that there was "everything there but a grand piano."

When Gaston Maspero, who happened to be in the Luxor area, and Davis poked their heads through a hole in the second doorway, they witnessed the most spectacular discovery ever made in the Valley until Tutankhamun's tomb eclipsed it seventeen years later. The burial chamber had been robbed but was largely undisturbed and awash with gold. A wooden sarcophagus with its lid removed contained three coffins, the innermost golden one holding the mummy of an elderly man. A complete chariot lay at the far end of the chamber. There were two beds, alabaster jars, and three gold-inlaid wooden armchairs. It was as if the mourning courtiers had set the furniture down and quietly departed. An inscription in gold on the sarcophagus identified the owners of the tomb as Yuya, a senior officer of Egyptian chariotry, and his wife Tuya. The couple received the great honor of burial among pharaohs because their daughter Tiye became the Great Royal Wife of Amenhotep III. Palm-sized marriage scarabs announcing the union and distributed in 1386 B.C. lay in the tomb.

After a celebratory lunch, Davis, Weigall, and Maspero returned to the tomb and began inventorying the contents. Davis studied Tuya's countenance until "her dignity and character so impressed me that I almost found it necessary to apologize for my presence."[7] He was so overcome by his thoughts that he fainted. The others carried him into the open air and revived him with brandy. The find was an international sensation. *The New York Times* hailed it as the greatest find in Egyptology, made at that by an American and a New Yorker. Davis became a celebrity, while the archaeologists continued to work in discreet anonymity. The excitement generated by the find created a fashion for things Ancient Egyptian. Tourists electrified by the pharaohs flocked to the Nile. Yuya and Tuya's burial caused major American museums to sponsor long-term research in Egypt for the first time.

Queen Tiye

All of this was a major turning point in the sorry archaeological history of the Valley of the Kings. David now became convinced that it was no use digging randomly in the Valley. Unlike others, who wanted instant gratification, Davis, who was no archaeologist in technical terms, had the self-control and the resources to dig for season after season with no guarantee of success. He set out to clear the sides of the Valley to bedrock.

Meanwhile, Howard Carter was in trouble. The Yuya discovery coincided with an unfortunate fracas at Saqqara, which involved a confrontation between Carter and a group of drunken French visitors.[8] The altercation turned violent, a complaint against Carter filed. Both Davis and Maspero urged him to express regret. The thin-skinned and obstinate Carter refused, was posted to a minor position, and resigned. He now eked out a precarious living as an artist and guide, while another archaeologist, Edward Ayrton, took over Davis's archaeology, on Wengell's recommendation.

Edward Russell Ayrton was an energetic twenty-three-year-old when he joined Davis in October 1905 with a two-year contract at £250 a year, equivalent to about $50,000 today. The son of a British diplomat in China with Petrie experience, he did not suffer fools. This was just as well in the demanding atmosphere of Valley excavations. Fortunately, Ayrton was an excellent organizer, who brought more order to Davis's research and never left the excavations. A few days after they started work, Davis noticed a large, tilted boulder. Ayrton dug around it with his hands and recovered a beautiful blue cup bearing the cartouche of a little known pharaoh, Tutankhamun. This was the first time Tutankhamun's name had appeared in the Valley. Further discoveries followed, including the robbed tomb of the XIX Dynasty pharaoh Siptah (ca.1195 B.C.), notable for its wall paintings (KV 47).

January 1907 saw the discovery of a stairway near the tomb of Ramesses IX (KV 6). At first, Ayrton thought a blank wall at its foot was an unfinished sepulcher, but more steps appeared beyond it. Rubble filled the corridor beyond almost to the ceiling, but Ayrton, Davis, and Weigall managed to crawl through and located parts of a shrine that had once covered the sarcophagus—just as one did in Tutankhamun's tomb. A limestone block nearby identified the wife of Amenhotep III, the mother of the pharaoh Akhenaten—Queen Tiye (KV 55). This unexpected discovery filled Davis with delight, for she was a queen of humble origins who had become the most powerful woman in Egypt. An almost Cleopatra-like aura soon surrounded the queen. The John Player Company even issued a cigarette card in her honor.

The three men managed to crawl beyond the shrine without damaging it. Twenty-one meters (70 feet) beyond lay the entry to the burial chamber and its gold covered inner and outer coffin. Gold shone on all sides, as bright as the day it was placed in the tomb. There was so much gold that it overshadowed the other artifacts in the tomb. Fragile artifacts and gold leaf started to fall apart directly the chamber was open; gold dust floated in the excavator's faces. Photography and sketching completed, Ayrton undertook the clearance of the sepulcher, the greatest challenge being the gold leaf inscriptions of the shrine. He treated them with paraffin to hold the gold in place, used wax and plaster of paris to record the inscriptions. When he removed the lid from the coffin, he had to remove eleven gold sheets that had once lined the coffin. The mummy lay in the traditional pose for Egyptian royal women, with her hands on her chest. The body was in bad shape and was roughly handled, so much of it crumbled to dust. Maspero had asked that the sepulcher be cleared rapidly, for he was apprehensive about robbery. Apparently, the removal was done carelessly. But one cannot entirely blame Davis or Ayrton. The technical challenges posed by the tomb were beyond the archaeological expertise of the day. The artist Harold Jones asked if he could take a handful of gold-laden dust from the floor. "Take two," Davis replied. Fifty years later, Jones's heirs gave the box and the dust with its gold fragments to the Swansea Museum in South Wales.

Davis and Emma Andrews were overwhelmed with visitors anxious to view the finds, which had been transferred to the *Beduin* for transport to Cairo. They became weary of the attention but tolerated a visit from Lord Cromer, the Consul General, and his wife. Lord and Lady Carnarvon appear in this narrative for the first time, for they visited the *dahabiyyah* to admire the Tiya finds. The two men did not get on well. Davis was far from bashful about his success. Carnarvon, much more understated and new to digging, had so far found nothing of importance.

While Davis basked in the public eye, disturbing reports of objects from the tomb being for sale in Luxor reached him. With typical decisiveness, he slipped across the river and purchased at least forty necklace fragments and a dozen gold pendants from the tomb for his collection. No one was arrested for stealing. Meantime, anatomist Elliot Grafton Smith examined Tiya's bones and declared they were those of a young man. Davis was livid, especially when Weigall, as inspector accepted Smith's conclusions. To this day, controversy surrounds Tiya's burial place. Most likely the sepulcher was opened at least twice to house other mummies.

"I Fear That the Valley of the Kings Is Now Exhausted"

Ayrton, who was about to leave to work elsewhere, now started work on the slope above Seti I's tomb. On December 21, he found a small pit about 91 meters (300 feet) from Tiya's tomb, full of sealed white jars. One cover was broken. Wrapped around it was a cloth bearing the name Tutankhamun. Dried wreaths and a small bag of a dusty substance lay nearby. The cloth referred to year six of Tutankhamun's reign. Ayrton and Davis put this find on one side and stored it as being of marginal importance. It was not until the early 1920s that Herbert Winlock of the Metropolitan Museum examined the artifacts closely and discovered they were relics of the embalming and burial of Tutankhamun.

In January, a mud-filled tomb came to light. Ayrton had to clear it with carving knives, a task that took days. He recovered a magnificent cache of gold objects, among them ear pendants, bracelets, rings, and filigree beads, including a pair of silver gloves for a small woman. The so-called Gold Tomb (KV 56) remains a mystery. It may have been a royal child's burial, once intact, then flooded by a heavy rainstorm. When Davis entertained Sir Eldon Gorst, the new Consul General after Lord Cromer, he is said to have torn apart ancient wreaths after dinner, angry because the jars in the tomb contained no gold.

If the discovery of KV 56 was not enough, Ayrton discovered another tomb, a twelve-step stairway leading into the hillside. An inscription on the wall identified it as the tomb of Horemheb (KV 57), the successor of Ay and Tutankhamun, whom we will meet later (Chapter 7). To explore the tomb, the party dragged themselves over rubble in stifling heat. Once they had crossed a decoy pit, they emerged in a burial chamber adorned with richly colored paintings. Horemheb's red granite sarcophagus and the paintings were photographed thoroughly and much admired. But there was no mummy.

Horemheb's unfinished tomb was Theodore Davis's last major discovery in the Valley. When he left, Ayrton and Weigall bickered constantly, the latter complaining that his colleague was possessive and "babyish," "a social affair." Much to Weigall's relief, Ayrton left to work with others. In 1911, he joined the Archaeological Survey of Ceylon (now Sri Lanka) and drowned on a shooting expedition in 1914.

Davis returned in 1909, but the excavations, headed this time by Harold Jones, were uneventful until a vertical shaft appeared in the valley floor. The fill contained all kinds of fragments, including cartouches of both Ay and Tutankhamun. A room filled with dried mud lay underneath, a single undecorated chamber that yielded twenty gold fragments also bearing the two pharaohs' names. Davis believed that the jars from KV 58 and the blue cup with Tutankhamun's name on it had been removed from what he believed to be his tomb. He was wrong.

At this point only two pharaohs' tombs were undiscovered—those of Tuthmosis II, still of unknown location, and the elusive Tutankhamun. Theodore Davis was slowing down. He found his last Valley tomb, his eighteenth, in 1910, but it was empty. In 1912, he wrote in his last monograph about Horemheb's tomb that "I fear that the Valley of the Kings is now exhausted."[9] *The New York Times* described Davis as "a greater detective than even Sherlock Holmes." *Punch* added that it understood that the matter "had been placed in the hands of the local police." Everyone agreed with

Davis except the obstinate, hardheaded Howard Carter. Davis relinquished his Valley concession and died in 1915.

History has been unkind to Theodore Davis. Once the fawning by the media ended, critics described him as careless and unscientific, the damage he wrought incalculable. Despite his remarkable discoveries—and they were both remarkable and important—he vanished rapidly into archaeological obscurity with the discovery of Tutankhamun's tomb in 1922. Only now, nearly a century later, is his work coming into broader focus. Unlike many of his contemporaries, he was generous to Egypt and left most of his most spectacular finds in the Cairo Museum, despite Maspero offering him more. His most important innovation was unspectacular, monotonous, and potentially unrewarding—stripping the Valley rubble to locate tombs. This he did with remarkable success.

Theodore Davis was the classic hands-off wealthy archaeologist, said to be "difficult to work for," who spent most of his time entertaining visitors rather than on the dig, although he was always present when a tomb was opened. He was lucky in his assistants—the incomparable Howard Carter, Edward Ayrton, and Arthur Weigall were all competent archaeologists with solid Egyptological credentials by the standards of the day. He also hired Harry Burton, the photographer who was to achieve immortality with his photographs of Tutankhamun's tomb. Even by the standards of the day, Theodore Davis was an unscrupulous robber baron, but such predatory behavior never extended to Egypt. Quite apart from his discoveries, Davis set research in the Valley of the Kings on a systematic, ultimately modern course. He and his archaeologists set the stage for the discovery of Tutankhamun's tomb. He came within a mere 2 meters (6 feet) of the sepulcher. Fortunately, he backed off out of fear of undermining the nearby track into the Valley.

Davis was already hard at work in the Valley of the Kings when another wealthy visitor decided to take up archaeology as a way of passing time during his winter visits. George Edward Stanhope Molyneaux Herbert, Fifth Earl of Carnarvon, had been a regular visitor to the Nile since 1889, had collected antiquities, but did not start digging until 1907. Two years later, Gaston Maspero teamed him up with the unemployed Howard Carter, who was convinced that Tutankhamun's tomb awaited discovery—and it did.

The story of archaeology's greatest discovery is well known, almost a cliché, but both Lord Carnarvon and Tutankhamun remain in the background. The former was Howard Carter's quiet sponsor, who tended to stay in the background. The young pharaoh remains a shadowy figure, despite the dissection of his tomb over the past century. What were they both really like? Were there any similarities in their characters, in their life experiences? Over the next few chapters, we'll unravel the complex tapestry that made up these two men's early lives, that came together when Carter and Carnarvon peered through a sealed doorway and saw "wonderful things." We begin with Tutankhamun.

Effective for the Aten

In late spring, 1349 B.C., the pharaoh Akhenaten announced his new capital. "On this day . . . His Majesty [appeared] on the great chariot of electrum . . . Setting [off] on a good road [toward] Akhetaten, his [the Aten's] place of creation, which he made for himself that he might set within it every day."[1] Surrounded by trotting soldiers, pharaoh Akhenaten made his first appearance at his new royal capital half way between the traditional administrative and religious capitals of Egypt—at Memphis and Thebes. The king's assembled courtiers made slavish obeisance, well aware that they were witnessing a momentous event. Many of them had worked for his father, Amenhotep III ("Amun is Content"), one of Egypt's greatest rulers. The youngest of Amenhotep's two sons, he became his successor when his older brother died. Akhenaten was educated in Memphis, the royal capital 320 kilometers (200 miles) downstream, where solar cults were a powerful presence.

Akhenaten had ascended to the throne in about 1351 B.C.. He was to reign for seventeen years.[2] The new pharaoh, at the time named Amenhotep IV, had impeccable dynastic credentials but soon caused shudders to ripple through the royal court. Ever since he was young, he had been mesmerized by the dazzling solar imagery at Thebes, with its spectacular, choreographed ceremonial. The king became obsessed with the brilliant orb of the sun, known as the Aten (or Aton). Now he had the power to change everything. He overturned religious orthodoxy and abandoned the ancient creator deity, Amun, the primordial god of hiddenness. In a dramatic symbolic move, Amenhotep IV changed his name to Akhenaten ("Effective for the Aten").

Centuries of traditional religious belief passed into near oblivion by pharaonic decree. Before the creation, the world had been a featureless sea (*nu*). Then a primordial mound rose from the waters, perhaps a symbolic depiction of the receding Nile inundation nourishing the land. Eight gods, known as the *Ogdoad*, presided over creation, among them the self-engendered deity Atum and his progeny, among them Ptah, the patron of craftspeople, and the transcendent god Amun. The theology varied from place to place, but that of Thebes proclaimed that Amun was the hidden force behind everything, fused with the primordial sun god to become Amun-Re, the supreme deity of the pantheon. Karnak, with its courts, colonnades, and columns, proclaimed the supremacy and might of Amun and the power and wealth of his priests. Amun's wife was Mut, goddess of fertility. There were, of course, other powerful deities, among them Osiris, whose wife Isis begat the falcon-headed god Horus, the god of war and hunting. Osiris presided over the afterlife, was the merciful judge of the dead in the afterlife, the granter of Nile floods and growing vegetation. The pharaohs were associated with Osiris in death. The Egyptians believed that their kings also rose from the dead and achieved immortality. In time, Amun merged with Horus as Re-Horakhty ("Horus of the Two Horizons") ruler of the sky, the earth, and the underworld.

Behind this elaborate and beloved pantheon lay *ma'at*, depicted as a goddess, a deeply cherished concept of truth, balance, and order, which set the order of the universe in the chaos at the moment of creation. The Egyptian cosmos with its serene order flourished in a brilliant interplay of air and light set within an endless wilderness of opaque waters. *Ma'at* was an ethical and moral principle in a society with a deep belief in cosmic harmony and tradition, as opposed to change. Since the unification of the Two Lands, pharaohs ruled by embracing *ma'at*—order in the face of chaos. Akhenaten's move appeared to threaten this most fundamental of all principles.

Under the new order, Re-Horakty, traditionally shown with a hawk's head, was identical to Aten, who was worshipped as a god rather than being merely an object— the Aten, the solar disk. Aten was now considered the sole ruling deity, known as "the living one, Re-Horakhty who rejoices on the horizon." He was not just the solar disk but also the life-giving illumination of the sun. He was the king of kings, with no queen, no threatening enemies. Aten was the only god, Akhenaten was his chosen prophet.

The pharaoh's precipitous shift to what can only be described as a fundamentalist theology sent violent shockwaves through Egypt's elite and the all-powerful, conservative priesthood of Amun. The symphony of chants and dances, of songs and offerings, ceased. The ancient temples fell silent and no longer honored their deities. Why he made the sudden move is unknown. Some experts believe he had escaped assassination at the hands of the priests of Amun or their agents, but this seems improbable. Most likely, he may have decided to centralize religious authority and enhance royal power, perhaps a response to pressure from below to erode royal religious prerogative and decorum. The pharaoh's draconian move spurred quiet talk of rebellion. With ill-concealed dissent on many sides, Akhenaten traveled everywhere surrounded by armed guards. He also declared that Aten himself had guided him to a new, hitherto unoccupied location for his capital, which he named Akhetaten, 400 kilometers (250 miles) downstream of Amun's temples at Thebes (Akhetaten is known to archaeologists as El-Amarna). Within the first decade of his reign, he eliminated, at least theoretically, all other deities from his domains.

"The Unique One of Re"

What was Akhenaten like? As did all pharaohs, he presided over a court of adoring sycophants. They described him as a teacher of righteous conduct. His writings are lost, except for the Hymn to the Aten, which he claimed to have written. The art style he perpetuated reveals a single-minded ruler who tried to make his people accountable for their conduct in the face of Aten. The pharaoh's artists depicted him as a long-faced man with sharp chin, narrow, almond-shaped eyes, full lips, a soft belly, and enlarged breasts. His peculiar appearance defies modern explanation. Some experts think he suffered from an inherited genetic condition known as Marfan's Syndrome, which produces physical features like those displayed by the pharaoh. He may, in fact, have had a normal appearance. Akhenaten called himself The Unique One of Re because Aten was the father and mother of humanity. Thus, artists depicted him as the living god on earth, androgynous, just like the god. It's worth noting that the more radical depictions date from early in his reign. Later portraits are more normal looking.

Of Akhenaten's character we know nothing, except for scenes of domestic harmony, which show the Aten's beams casting light on the pharaoh and his wife with their young children. He may have been kind, he may have been a brave warrior, for all we know. We can be certain, however, from his public pronouncements, that he

Figure 3.1   Akhenaten and Nefertiti. *From Gerbil from de.wikipedia.*

was decisive when it came to his religious beliefs and his image of his sacred capital. The pharaoh was obsessed with Aten. Everyone else mortal was supposed to worship the king as a living god. Judging from statuettes in the city's houses, most people quietly continued worshipping the traditional deities.

The king's charioteer drew up in an open space before a dazzling white inscription in the rock face of the cliffs behind his new city. Akhenaten dismounted and joined his queen, Nefertiti, now known as Neferneferuaten ("Beauteous Are the Beauties of the Aten") before a lavish regiment of offerings to Aten—"bread, beer, long-and short-horned cattle . . . all finds of fresh green plants everything good."[3] After some prayers, the royal couple took their seats on ornate thrones under a shady awning. The thin-faced, slender pharaoh with protruding lips addressed his courtiers with formal, choreographed words:

> I shall make Akhetaten for the Aten, my father, in this place, he announced. He described the stelae that would mark the boundaries of the holy city, which he would build for the Sun God.

> I shall make the "House of the Aten" for the Aten, my father, in Akhetaten. I shall make the "Mansion of the Aten" for the Aten, my father, . . . I shall make the Sun Temple of the Great King's Wife [Neferneferuaten-Nefertiti] . . . in this place.[4]

Then he made an announcement that must have sent shivers of apprehension through his courtiers.

> I shall make for myself the apartments of Pharoah, I will make the apartments of the Great King's Wife in Akhetaten.[4]

In other words, the deserted but spectacular semicircle of fertile land and cliffs would become the capital of his kingdom, known to Egyptians as *Kmt*, the Black Land, because of its dark, fertile soil. To leave no one in any doubt of his commitment, he also ordered that the tombs for himself, his wife, and family be built in the eastern cliffs near his new capital.

With this proclamation, Akhenaten defined the lives of his family, born and as yet unborn, as well as the careers of the powerful men who ruled Egypt in his shadow and watched his every move. Three massive tableaux cut into the rocks at the northern and southern boundaries of the site recorded both ceremony and proclamation. Statues of the pharaoh and his queen adorned each marker. A year later, the king returned once again in his electrum chariot and spent the night in a carpeted tent named "Aten is content." At dawn he rode out, made further lavish offerings, and swore an oath to the deity that everything in his capital was the god's and issued a second decree establishing the city limits with greater precision.

Tutankhaten Is Born

The pharaoh's architects laid out Akhetaten as a royal capital that gave prominence to the major public buildings, built in a short time along the so-called Royal Road that ran north and south along the river front.[5] Akhenaten, Nefertiti, and their six children lived in the North Palace, sited between the cliffs and the river for security reasons. The palace lay within a fortified enclosure, together with a large administrative building, houses for important officials, and barracks for the garrison. Hitherto, wives and families had stayed in the background, even when consorts played important roles in the affairs of state. Akhenaten turned his wife and children into a holy family. Statues of Akhenaten and Nefertiti adorned every public building. The pharaoh and his queen were now divine representatives on earth, intermediaries to the gods, whose statues they had now replaced with their own. Akhenaten watched over everybody; everyone was to worship him, even in their household shrines. The pharaoh *was* Egypt.

The North Palace, like all Akhetaten's public buildings, stage-managed the divine being, whether it be a deity or the pharaoh. The king and his family lived in isolated splendor behind the walls of the palace. His subjects rarely saw him, except when he was riding his chariot or presiding over a reward ceremony for esteemed officials at a Window of Appearance built into the palace wall. There was a small throne room as well, where the pharaoh received trusted advisors in private. But the North Palace with its lush gardens was, above all, the royal residence, where Akhenaten and his family enjoyed as much privacy as an Egyptian ruler could expect, surrounded as they were by fawning officials, guards, and servants. It was here, in this guarded palace, that the pharaoh' son, Tutankhaten ("Living Image of Aten"), was born in 1333 or 1331 B.C.* All we know of his birth is a newborn's tunic of red and white stripes from his tomb bearing the embroidered cartouche of Akhenaten, dated to year seven of the pharaoh's reign. The mourners wrapped the tunic around the sculpture of the jackal god Anubis, who guarded the so-called Treasury (for tomb plan, see Chapter 10).

Tutankhaten's mother remains somewhat of a mystery. Perhaps she was Nefertiti, or Akhenaten's secondary wife Kiya, or someone else.[6] Of Nefertiti, The Great Royal Wife, we know little except for the exquisite bust of the queen in all her ceremonial finery found in an Amarna sculptor's workshop. Whether this high-cheeked portrait reflects the real person, we do not know. She was certainly a competent woman, who had a considerable say in state affairs, perhaps even ruling briefly as Neferneferuaten as a coregent after her husband's death—the controversy still continues (see Chapter 5).

Inbreeding was a long tradition in the Egyptian royal family, which had unfortunate consequences for a significant number of its members, including the newborn

---

*I use the name Tutankhaten in the narrative until the young king changed it to Tutankhamun after his accession.

prince. He came into the world with a congenital deformity, a birth defect known as clubfoot. Found in young males, the muscle tissues to the bones are shorter than normal, causing the foot to twist. Today, clubfoot can be cured during early childhood, but Tutankhaten had to walk on the side of his left foot. He probably used walking sticks much of the time, although this is debated. One hundred and thirty sticks came from his tomb, one of them a reed set into a golden handle. The inscription thereon reads "a reed which his majesty cut with his own hand." He was also born with a minor cleft palate. With these and other disabilities, the prince was frail from birth. Thin faced and slender, probably with somewhat spindly legs, Tutankhaten was not an imposing child.

An Orchestrated Childhood

Judging from written sources from other reigns, he was born in a special birthing room, then handed over to a royal wet nurse named Maia, a member of the nobility.[7] If normal custom prevailed, known to us from a book of wisdom known as *The Papyrus of Ani*, she would have suckled Tutankhaten for three years. This kept the infant away from contaminated water, which improved his chances of survival. Among other honorifics, Maia bore the title "educator of the king's body." We know nothing about her life, but the pharaoh appears seated on her lap on the wall of her tomb. She must have been the first close relationship of Tutankhaten's life and may still have been around court when he became king. Similarly, Lord Carnarvon spent much of his childhood in the company of nannies and trusted servants.

Tutankhaten grew up just like other royal children.[8] We know little about them, thanks to the orgy of destruction that followed Akhenaten's death. He had six sisters or half-sisters. Of the six, the eldest, Mereyaten married Smenkhare and may also have served as her father's Great Chief Wife after the death of Nefertiti. Another sister, Ankhesenpaaten, married Tutankhaten.

The royal young spent their days in the *kap*—the Ancient Egyptian equivalent of a nursery. *Kaps* were guarded, isolated, and secure places. Few people entered this area of the private quarters, except doctors, nurses, entertainers, and tutors. Excavations have shown that the North Palace had a sunken garden in its central court, nourished by a well. Numerous chambers painted with brightly colored birds flying among papyrus reeds adorned the walls. A bed recess at the rear of the chambers allowed royal women and their children to take siestas on hot afternoons. The palace had an aviary and possibly even an area where larger animals lived in captivity. The royal children grew up in an idyllic environment, surrounded by birds and bright colors. Shallow pools and water plants adorned the gardens, where the young Tutankhaten might have tried to catch fish. Even when he was very young, he would have been familiar with prey that he would hunt in later life.

Figure 3.2 The young Tutankhaten modeled on a stopper. © *Griffith Institute, University of Oxford.*

Few people received an education alongside the royal prince. Those that did were from the highest ranks of the elite and considered it a major honor for the rest of their lives. Princely hostages from other lands also lived and were brought up here. To be known as a "child of the royal nursery" was a sign that you enjoyed a close bond with royal princes. Such a bond, like the one Tutankhaten forged with his playmates, were the foundations of the close trust that strengthened a pharaoh's power in later life. In a somewhat similar manner, Lord Carnarvon's childhood friends and contacts were the baseline of his later life.

If normal practice was followed, and there is no reason to believe that it was not, Tutankhaten would have started his formal education at about age four. Akhenaten appointed Count Sennedjem, Fan-Bearer on the Right of the King, a title that implied he had the ear of the pharaoh, and Overseer of Tutors, as royal tutor, to supervise the prince until adulthood.[9] We know little about this well-connected courtier, but he must have been a major influence on his charge, who remained associated with him even when Tutankhaten ascended the throne. Sennedjem's much-vandalized tomb bears an inscription in which he is seen riding alongside then-pharaoh Tutankhamun in his chariot, a clear sign of royal favor.

Figure 3.3 Tutankhamun's writing palette. © *Griffith Institute, University of Oxford.*

Like all royal princes, Tutankhaten lived a controlled life, orchestrated by precedents that had been in place for centuries. His education, either in the North Palace or in the House of Life, the archive and school within the enclosure of the King's House, resembled that of scribes, who learned their craft in special schools, as well as preparing him for a career in the administration, the military, or the priesthood.[10] Every ruler was literate, in an era when literacy was a key to power—power over information. An ability to write meant that a pharaoh could correspond with foreign rulers in his own hand, a useful asset in a world where personal relationships and kin ties were foundations of leadership and government.

We know Tutankhaten was literate. Fifteen scribal palettes of various sizes came from the tomb, some still bearing traces of ink. One was an artist's palette, which could hold six colors. Some were portable. A golden reed holder once held his reed pens. He even had a burnishing tool for smoothing the surfaces of papyrus documents. Whether or not he made his own paper is questionable, but palettes hint that he was a bright child, eager to learn. Tutankhaten would have begun by learning hieratic script, the cursive hieroglyphs used in day-to-day government business. That was enough for most scribes, but princes, who could perhaps become pharaoh, would become the highest priest in Egypt, so they also had to learn the formal hieroglyphs that adorned sepulchers and temples.

Mastering scripts was just the beginning. As did humble scribes, Tutankhaten would have memorized Egypt's classic literature, including wisdom texts such as the *Maxims of Ptahhotep*, common sayings dating back tens of centuries. Proclaimed the learned sage: "Great is Ma'at, and its foundation is established. It has not been shaken since the time of Osiris."[11] Ma'at, the Egyptian sense of rightness and order, was the most fundamental principle of pharaonic rule. In an interesting coincidence, Ptah-hotep's sayings appear on the celebrated Carnarvon Tablet, one of the Earl's very first archaeological finds over three thousand years later.

A prince had far more to learn than even the most important scribe, for he had to absorb the responsibilities of kingship. *The Teachings for King Merikare,* written by an unknown official for the pharaoh of that name a thousand years earlier, gave sound advice.[12] The anonymous author stressed the vital importance of oratory: "Be skillful in speech that you may be strong; it is the strength of the tongue, and words are braver than all fighting."

A wise pharaoh ruled with precedents from earlier reigns: "Copy your forefathers, for [work] is carried out through knowledge."

Judicious, careful governance depended on respect for one's subjects and concern for their safety. One also treated high officials with dignity, reinforced with rewards. This was, of course, strict self-interest. "Make your magnates great, that they may execute your law."

Show respect for Aten and other gods, maintain justice, pay careful attention to precedent and the deeds of one's forebears—the advice given to Merikare passed down the generations to become a secular version of Holy Writ drummed into Tutankhaten's head.

By the time he was seven, young Tutankhaten had absorbed a considerable array of knowledge, commonplace and esoteric, public and secret, also mythic, in preparation for possible kingship. He had also received some military training and seems to have developed a passion for chariots and hunting. We know he rode horses from the five-fingered gloves and two-fingered gauntlets used for chariot driving that accompanied him to eternity. Some could only have been worn by a young boy, so he obviously mounted horses and chariots early in life. Reliefs show him driving a small chariot in a royal procession. He would also have learned to swim when very young.

We can be sure that great care was taken with Tutankhaten's education, despite his obvious frailty. The stakes were enormous. He lived in an era of short life expectancy, where everyone, whether pharaoh, high official, or humble villager, could die at any moment. Medical care was rudimentary, there were no antibiotics, and epidemics of such inflictions as bubonic plague could kill thousands of people in weeks. A cemetery of common folk in a desert valley near Akhetaten contains at least 3,000 people. Seventy percent of a sample of 200 of them died before age 36.[13] Many of them suffered from malnutrition in childhood, others from pathologies caused by hefting weighty loads. The threat of sudden death always weighed on pharaonic courts; the ruler, but also royal princes, could die at a moment's notice, placing the succession in doubt.

For centuries, factionalism and jostling for position among royal siblings and high courtiers vying for favor and power simmered under the formal and ordered life of the Egyptian court. Akhenaten's was no different, the tension heightened by the pharaoh's obsessive devotion to Aten. Tutankhaten may have spent his childhood in isolation, but the time was approaching when he would appear in public in the presence of the pharaoh. The king's daughters might take formal precedence over the frail young prince, but everyone was aware that he could well become the future pharaoh.

Aten's City

Aten's city rose in a magnificent setting on the east bank of the Nile, where a fertile floodplain lay opposite a secluded, natural amphitheater bounded by precipitous, spectacular cliffs.[14] No one lived in this defendable location, where, we are told, the very shape of the cliffs formed the hieroglyph "horizon," over which the sun's orb, Aten, appeared every day.

Akhenaten's capital has long been a magnet for archaeologists. Napoléon's savants prepared the first detailed map of Akhetaten in 1798–1799 and published it in the *Description de l'Égypte*. John Gardner Wilkinson worked at the site in 1824, as did the German scholar Richard Lepsius in 1843 and 1845. He published an improved map of the city that recorded many now-vanished features. Twenty-two years later, an Egyptian woman stumbled across a cache of over 300 cuneiform tablets, the diplomatic correspondence now known as the Amarna Letters. The discovery brought Flinders Petrie to the site for a season in 1891. He worked with his characteristic speed, excavating test pits in the Great Temple of the Aten, several palaces, official buildings, and private houses. He unearthed more tablets, glass factories, and evidence of foreign trade—Mycenaean potsherds from mainland Greece in the palace garbage heaps. His excavators included Howard Carter. Between 1905 and 1914, German archaeologist Ludwig Borchardt excavated in the suburbs. He recovered the iconic bust of Queen Nefertiti, which now resides in Berlin. Controversy surrounds its export, for he may have claimed it was an artifact made of gypsum. British Egyptologist Barry Kemp has been working at the site since 1977. His work forms the basis for the descriptions of Akhenaten in these pages.

The principal construction took about two years, much of the stone coming from huge quarries in the northern cliffs, construction helped by using blocks small enough to be carried by a single worker. The pharaoh moved there in 1364 B.C. Hundreds of laborers worked to build the Royal Road, which ran parallel to the Nile. This was the ceremonial spine of the city that linked the northern parts of Akhetaten and the

North Palace with the "House of the Aten," the great temple, and the nearby Great Palace and a smaller temple, "The Mansion of the Aten." The Royal Road was a symbolic highway. The pharaoh rode along it in his chariot from his residence to where he governed. Akhenaten's short journey replicated the journey of the Aten through the heavens, the act of a divine king ruling alongside his deity in the heavens.

The administrative hub of Akhetaten centered on the House of Aten with its two massive pylons and huge open courts. The façade fronted the Road for about 300 meters (750 feet) and extended back about 0.8 kilometer (1/2 mile). Small earthen altars dotted the courtyards for the numerous food offerings for the god, to be consumed by him as he passed overhead. Just the logistics needed to slaughter animals and provide grain and fruit for the altars beggar the imagination. The pharaoh conducted the business of state in the King's House next door, with its balcony for public appearances by the royal family.

A covered bridge linked the administrative quarters with the Great Palace, a massive structure covering 1.6 hectares (almost 4 acres). The palace was a setting for the grand ceremonies, receptions, and orchestrated royal appearances that marked much of the year. Here formal state business unfolded in a huge open court adorned with larger-than-life statues of Akhenaten and Nefertiti. The effect was calculated to impress and terrify both high officials and visiting emissaries from other nations. The pharaoh walked on a plastered floor painted with images of foreigners. He trampled on his enemies as he personified the most powerful state in Egypt's world.

A smaller structure, The Mansion of the Aten, just to the south, served as the temple for the royal family's routine worship. Aligned with a cleft in the cliffs, it also served as a mortuary temple. With their open courts and sequences of ramps, steps, and balustrades, Akhetaten's public buildings embraced a new form of architecture that allowed people to worship the sun in the heavens, a far cry from the much more closed chambers of Amun's long-established temples in Thebes and elsewhere. It somewhat resembles what is known of Re's temples at Heliopolis in lower Egypt, for Re was, after all, one of Aten's manifestations.

No one knows how many people lived in the city, but an intelligent estimate is in the order of 30,000, of whom about 10 percent were members of the elite.[15] Except for the central precincts and outlier palaces, it was an agglomeration of what one might call urban villages, centered on the residences of officials, who in turn maintained broader connections within the city and much farther afield. Much of Akhetaten was a hive of factories producing all manner of commodities for temples and palaces—pottery and glass, vases and ornaments. The city was especially well known for its faience, widely used for beads and small statuettes. (Ancient Egyptian faience was a sintered quartz ceramic that created a blue-green luster.) There were sculptors and painters, weavers and all kinds of specialized artisans, often clustered in their own village-like quarters, just like the tomb workers' village at Deir el-Medina in the Theban Necropolis. This was a city that existed for the Aten and his divine representative on earth, one where the vizier's office kept a record of everyone, yet a place where everyone still maintained at least slight connections with their home villages, many some distance away. Even after thousands of years of pharaonic rule, Egypt was a civilization of rural villages.

In the final analysis, places like Akhetaten were large, often informal networks of people who lived in small-scale localities, often huddled close to the Royal Road. At the pinnacle sat the vizier, the intermediary between the pharaoh and his government. He oversaw an inner circle of high officials in an atmosphere of sycophancy and suspicion that assessed even the most trivial gesture or utterance. One watched what one said, what one did, and paid careful attention to the shifting sands of different court factions. All of this lay at the king's feet, a ruler who governed by precedent and with divine guidance. Unchanging routine, rigid protocol, abject obeisance, and intense scrutiny shaped every pharaoh's life. The young Tutankhaten became part of this royal theater from infancy, just as Lord Carnarvon became enmeshed in the formality of the London Season and other aristocratic social functions.

The Lord of Appearances

Akhenaten stood motionless in his magnificent chariot as he passed northward along the Royal Road. He looked straight ahead, oblivious to the people clustered along the roadside. A regiment of soldiers and policemen, spears at the ready, trotted alongside, some ahead of the king, others to either side. The chariot glistened in the sunlight, the matched horses groomed to perfection, their plumed heads held high. A short time before, the hot, dusty road had been busy with the routine travels of the city. Laden donkeys brayed under heavy loads. Markets away from the river pulsed with colorful activity. Men and women gossiped and haggled over vegetables. Potters turned clay vessels in shaded workshops. Then soldiers swept everyone off the highway. A dust cloud appeared to the south. The pharaoh swept by at speed, without looking at the mud brick houses and crowded alleyways on either side. Few folk paused to stare at what was a familiar sight, something quite different from the great religious festivals that were formal spectacles. Those that did made obeisance to the divine king.

The chariot entered the imposing courtyard facing the Great Palace. Bright streamers on tall poles greeted the pharaoh. The vizier and other high officials stood waiting his arrival. Soldiers clustered around as the king entered the huge building and vanished from public view. This was how it should be. Egyptian rulers lived isolated lives, distant from the gaze of common folk. They appeared only on formal occasions, unless moving from one part of their domains to another. Even then, they traveled by boat along the Nile, distanced from the towns and rural communities on either bank.

Today was a day of rewards, of gifts to high officials for their service. There were fixed wages, calculated in units of grain in Egypt, part of a complex system of payment in kind that extended from the pharaoh himself down to humble villagers. Everyone depended on the divine ruler, the living personification of the Sun God Aten. It was he who distributed lavish gifts to his closest advisors and officers. They, in turn, passed on some of the pharaoh's bounty and their own to their loyal followers. In a city such as Akhetaten, power emanated from the person of the pharaoh in formal appearances, in his audiences for foreign dignitaries, or when he emerged at the Window of Appearance in his palaces.

For some time, the chariots of high officials had delivered courtiers to the palace. They assembled in the great courtyard within, hidden from public view. Guards checked them as the pharaoh's herald marshaled them by rank. Then they waited in silence. Among them was Count Sennedjem, Fan-Bearer on the Right of the King and Overseer of Tutors. Beside him, leaning on an inlaid wooden stick, was Akhenaten's eldest son, 7-year-old Tutankhaten, attending a formal royal event for the first time.

"Effective for the Aten" appeared, accompanied by his wife Nefertiti. He wore a fine linen tunic, decorated with intricate tapestry. An elaborate flax sash woven in multiple colors bore the king's name and a reference to the year of his reign. He wore the formal crown with its hissing cobra, the age-old symbol of a unified Two Lands—Upper and Lower Egypt. The flail and crook of kingship crossed in his hands. Nefertiti's long, fine woven gown extended to her ankles. She wore a helmet-like crown cap adorned with a golden diadem, with a *uraeus*, the sacred cobra and symbol of royalty, over her brow. Neither king nor queen looked left or right as they progressed through the lines of prostrated courtiers, foreheads to the floor. Even the royal daughters and Tutankhaten paid homage. The watchful Sennedjem, resplendent in his official regalia, stood next to the diminutive prince. The young heir turned his head a little and peered out at the passing pharaoh. "He's getting restless," thought Sennedjem. "This restlessness must be checked."

The pharaoh, The Lord of Appearances, and his queen appeared without warning at the Window of Appearance with its ornate frame. They looked down on a large crowd, silenced by the sudden glimpse of the king. A row of soldiers guarded the steps and kept everyone at a distance. A row of officials stood to one side, waiting to be called for their moment in the spotlight. Leaning across an embroidered cushion, Akhenaten announced promotions and tossed down lavish gifts for each recipient to catch and pile on the ground. Much of the gifting was in jewelry—collars, necklaces, signet rings, and armlets—but there were bulkier, more prosaic commodities such as gloves, stools, and wine-filled amphorae, also baskets and bags of grain, even cattle, received separately. On this occasion, God's Father, the trusted advisor Ay and his wife Tey, received the king's bounty. Ay donned a pair of linen gloves and a gold collar. His overjoyed retainers carried away the lavish gifts. "Look at that stool and that bag," called out one underling, "They have become people of gold." Everyone in Ay's retinue would benefit from the gifting, a calculated way of assuring his loyalty to pharaoh and Aten.

The ceremony unfolded at a deliberate, mind-numbing pace, enlivened by the joyous behavior of happy followers. Courtiers stood motionless in the pharaoh's presence. Tutankhaten soon became bored. He leant on his stick, for his leg was painful. He fidgeted, scratched himself, looked upward, and to the side.

"Be still, boy," hissed Sennedjem, resisting a temptation to cuff his restless charge. "Remember who you are."

Tutankhaten froze in place.

Chapter 4

A Gambler with Enthusiasms

Windsor Racecourse, England, 1884. The three boys, one pale and English and two swarthy Indians, clambered over the low fence and pushed their way through the jostling crowd. Elegant gentlemen in top hats rubbed shoulders with check-coated farmers and red-faced, overweight businessmen reeking of beer. Touts nudged reluctant gamblers and whispered temptations in their ears. Drunken laborers staggered through the crowd, edging their way to the bookies' stalls with a few pence in their hands. A loud cacophony of sounds assaulted the ears—meat pie sellers advertising their wares, young men arguing over a bet, older gentlemen discussing the entries in the next race. A smell of stale beer, gin, sweat, and horse dung eddied over the crowd.

"Come on," urged Victor Singh, pushing his long hair back from his forehead. "There's not much time."

Victor's brother and Porchy, Lord Porchester—soon to become Lord Carnarvon—slender, hesitant, and nervous, followed close behind him, holding onto their money, well aware that pickpockets operated in the crowd. They watched as the suave Victor placed their bets with a bookie, who greeted him with a smile. His client was a lavish gambler, who lost more than he won.

After the last race, the threesome slipped back to school undetected, several pounds poorer.

An Aristocrat Is Born

Porchy and Tutankhaten: two parallel lives. The one found the other 3,300 years after he died. Both enjoyed lives of extraordinary privilege. Both suffered from chronic ill health and were isolated from the outside world for years. Aristocrat and pharaoh: both rebelled against different straightjackets—of social convention and religious conformity. Nothing in Porchy's early life even hinted at archaeology. How did an indolent nobleman with a disastrous education develop a sense of adventure and curiosity, and a decisiveness that was alien to others' perceptions of him? Why did he become obsessed with Tutankhamun?

George Edward Stanhope Molyneux Herbert, son of the Fourth Earl of Carnarvon, was born on Tuesday, June 26, 1866, at 66 Grosvenor Street, a fashionable London precinct. He was born into a year when assassins tried to kill the Russian Tsar and Otto Von Bismarck, when root beer and the urinal were patented, and a year after the American Civil War ended. The curly-haired, slightly built Porchy was a weak child from the outset, plagued by poor health. His infancy followed predictable, aristocratic custom. Nannies took over his care and feeding, their realm the nursery. This mother, the countess, was a busy political hostess, who spent little time with her children.[1] One is reminded of Tutankhamun's *kap*.

In 1879, at age thirteen, Porchy entered Eton College near Windsor, west of London, the school of choice for Britain's elite, many of them the heirs to great estates.[2] He was frail, thin, and withdrawn, bullied and often sick, an outsider until he became friends with Victor Duleep Singh, the son of an Indian maharajah from the Punjab, who was a friend of Edward, the Prince of Wales. Short and longhaired, with a complexion described by a newspaper as "olive . . . not darker than an Italian," he was more British than the British, with an aristocratic passion for gambling, at the time a fashionable pursuit. Victor had caused a sensation early on by having the audacity to lay a bet of five pounds against a horse with the Eton equivalent of God—the Captain of Boats. He won.

Porchy was, of course, familiar with gambling. He could be nothing else, given how much of his family's life revolved around horseflesh. Perhaps he met Victor in a small workshop at the back of a hosier's in town named Brown's. Here, a grave-looking, white-haired old man named Solomon spent his days ironing top hats and handing out priceless tips on racehorses. Impecunious Lower School boys flocked to listen to him, but Victor was another matter. He had the money and used Solomon's tips to good effect. The two boys took to one another at once—the quiet Lord Porchester and the effervescent Indian, whose entrepreneurial personality meant that he took the lead. Socially adept, charming, and handsome, Victor, like Porchy, had received little affection or attention from his parents. Both had harsh fathers; neither was very clever. They became inseparable, lifelong friends, as well as compulsive gamblers.

Porchy and Victor would slip away from school and bet at the nearby Royal Windsor Racecourse. They even went as far afield as Ascot Races, were sometimes caught and punished, but they persisted. When they lost, they borrowed money from bookkeeper's agents and moneylenders in London. It was a matter of time before disturbing stories of their escapades reached the school authorities and the ears of Porchy's high-minded father. Furious, he removed Porchy from Eton and Victor's company in 1881 and sent him in disgrace to a lonely exile at Highclere Castle, the Carnarvon seat near Newbury.

Highclere Castle with its huge estate has acquired fame as the backdrop for the *Downton Abbey* television series, which depicts the fortunes of a wealthy landowning

Figure 4.1   Highclere Castle. *From JB + UK_Planet via FlickR*.

family before World War I and beyond. The castle has a long history, being trans-formed into a grand mansion by the Third Earl in 1838, the interior being finally completed in 1876, when Highclere became a center of late Victorian political life in the hands of the Fourth Earl and his wife. The saloon and library are justly famous, the former boasting of leather wall coverings from Spain installed in 1862. So is the draw-ing room, decorated with green French silk given to Almina Carnarvon by Alfred de Rothschild in 1895. The castle is the "set" for *Downton Abbey*, but the characters bear, of course, no resemblance to the generations of Carnarvons who have lived there. A visit to Highclere, as well as the TV series does, however, give one a flavor of what the aristocratic life of the Fifth Earl and Countess was like. It was expensive, lavish, and completely over the top by today's standards. The Fifth Earl's Egyptian collection was sold to the Metropolitan in New York after his death to pay death duties. Some artifacts remained but were stored until rediscovered by the family in 1987 and are exhibited in the house. The Egyptian government demanded their return, but unsuc-cessfully. (In a nice footnote, the yellow labrador that features in the beginning credits of *Downton Abbey* is named Isis, in a subtle nod to the associations between Ancient Egypt, the Carnarvons, and Highclere.)

Lord and Lady Carnarvon lived at the pinnacle of British society. They presided over what can be described as a patriarchal, near feudal series of estates, apparently with considerable benevolence. Again, parallels to the pharaoh's court come to mind, if far-fetched. The Fourth Earl attended Eton and Oxford University, entered politics, and became Secretary of State for the Colonies at age twenty-seven, a post in which he excelled. But he was diffident and shy, was plagued with ill health and not gifted with social graces. The Earl was a staunch conservative, blessed with the nickname of "Twitters." A cultured, high-achieving man, he expected the same of his children—a dedication to the family and service to the Crown. His wife, a noted beauty, was a brilliant hostess but also suffered from serious health problems. The journalist Walter Bageshot, who had connections in the highest circles, described them as "being *people*." Being *people* meant keeping your children in the background.

Every Egyptian pharaoh worried about the succession, about having sons to inherit the throne. Death stalked their palaces, striking down even the healthy with little notice. Their courts teemed with plotting factions ready to cash in on sudden death, if the heir apparent was unhealthy. Like Akhenaten's court, Highclere Castle was haunted by ill health, with uncertainties about the future, with an apparently frail male heir in prospect, whose survival to adulthood was uncertain. With their wealth and enormous real estate holdings, the Carnarvons also faced high stakes, knowing that Lady Evelyn suffered from weak lungs and chronic ill health. Porchy, who was a frail child, lived under a formal, chilly regime, brought up largely by nurses and governesses, His mother died suddenly when he was nine.[3] The Earl remarried, this time his 33-year-old cousin, Elizabeth Catherine Howard. Their eldest son, Aubrey Herbert, was born in 1880, but he was also frail, perhaps, like the pharaohs, because of inbreeding.

The oldest son's schooling was a disaster from the beginning.[4] One suspects that he had undiagnosed learning disabilities such as dyslexia or Attention Deficit Disorder (ADD), but nothing was known about such conditions in his day. This would explain his apparent revulsion for formal learning from an early age. His two-year Eton career was dismal, apart from his gambling. Now the Earl aimed Porchy at Oxford. A strict cramming regime was called for. He was sent to Embleton Vicarage between Edinburgh and Newcastle. Here, Mandall Creighton, a strict clergyman and future Bishop of London, prepared aristocratic sons for Oxford University. The spartan institution housed older males whose confidence far outweighed that of the seventeen-year-old Porchester. He was shy, not a good scholar, and bullied. Embleton gave him little, except an addiction to cigarette smoking, acquired from Creighton, who rolled cigarettes for his pupils. His application to Balliol College, Oxford, faltered, so his father urged the army as an alternative. He sent him to Captain Walter James, a London crammer who specialized in getting boys through the Sandhurst Military Academy. Once again, he rebelled and abandoned his studies, pleading ill health. In truth, he felt suffocated by the constant studying, by his persistent academic failures, craved Victor's company, and missed his true passions—horseracing, sailing, shooting, and traveling.

Porchy Becomes the Earl

Porchy's life turned slowly for the better after he inherited two large estates, some coal mines, and a London residence from his grandmother, which made him richer, on paper, than his father. Aristocratic privilege gained him admission to Trinity College, Cambridge, but, deeply in debt, he was sent down for academic reasons after a year.

By this time, Lord Carnarvon refused to support his son any more. Father and mother took off for Australia, while Porchy embarked on an extended voyage across the Atlantic to Rio de Janeiro on a 110-foot yacht, the *Aphrodite,* in 1887. His quiet, withdrawn personality reveled in the experience. He spent long hours reading, acquiring a compulsive taste for books that became a mainstay of his life. Some years later, he said that he was fond of horse racing and automobiles, but would rather stay in a comfortable chair if another absorbing book fell into his hands. He educated himself with omnivorous reading in everything from art and the classics to political thought. His reading also stimulated his curiosity and his taste for the exotic and unusual. Carnarvon became a classic autodidact. The voyage was an invaluable experience that exposed him at an impressionable age to other cultures, other lands, and gave him a taste for modest adventure. According to his sister, Lady Winifred Burghclere, who wrote an appreciation of him, Porchy was "a bibliophile, a collector of china and drawings, and indeed of all things rare and beautiful, with a fine taste intensified by observation and study."[5] His interest in collecting art and antiques was to attract him to Egyptian antiquities.

Back in London, Porchy resumed his frivolous escapades with Victor. But he had toned down. He was still shy, but was also quieter, softer spoken, and calmer. Lacking Victor's social graces, he shunned many invitations and was often boorish when forced to be sociable. Instead, he withdrew more and more from his family and London society. He continued to travel abroad, going upcountry on an African hunting expedition in 1888. Many years later, Lady Winifred Burghclere recalled a memorable hunt where he hid in the bush, got a shot at an elephant, missed, and then sauntered across a large clearing. The beast stalked him, and then charged. Porchy took to his heels, threw away his rifle and ammunition, and climbed a tree out of harm's way. He stayed as far away from his parents, too, despite being far from well. But he was fit enough to travel to Egypt for the first time in 1889, when he enjoyed the fleshpots of Cairo without, apparently, showing much interest in archaeology. Despite his poor health, he also traveled out to Australia and then returned via East Asia and North America. By the time he reached London, his father was in the terminal stages of liver cancer. Lord Porchester realized he was about to become the Fifth Earl of Carnarvon. He dreaded the inheritance, the endless social regimentation, the dreary public ceremonies and formal banquets that seemed to be the lot of landed aristocracy (and, in a different way, of a pharaoh). He made but one concession to his father, allowing himself to be presented at court two weeks before the Earl died on June 28, 1890.

Figure 4.2 Almina Carnarvon.
© *Victoria and Albert Museum, London.*

Porchy was twenty-four years old when he presided over his father's obsequies and became the Fifth Earl of Carnarvon. All the heavy responsibilities of the title descended on his ill-prepared shoulders. His health was precarious. He was deeply in debt with encumbered properties on every side. Nevertheless, he persisted in his travels across Europe and threw large shooting parties at Highclere. By 1894, however, Porchy's and Victor's bachelor days were drawing to a close. Victor, as an army officer, needed a wife. So did Porchy, given his heavy responsibilities as head of the family. In a last fling, they went on a yachting trip in the Carnarvon yacht, the *Katarina*, and played the tables at Cannes and Monte Carlo. On the face of it, Porchy was an attractive marital prospect, despite his enormous debts from gambling and his dubious associations with shady characters in London's club life and elsewhere. He was not a good-looking man, and his years of dissipation had aged him considerably. But he had one priceless asset. Whoever married him would become a countess and a member of Britain's exclusive aristocracy. After a few months of courtship, the Earl became engaged to Almina Victoria Marie Alexandra Wombwell (1876–1969).

The future countess had spent much of her youth in Paris, where she moved in rarified social circles.[6] There she met Alfred Charles de Rothschild (1842–1918), a wealthy and eccentric banker with a passion for art. He became a beloved and trusted guardian to a very attractive, socially ambitious woman. Almina moved in the highest levels of London society, where she met Carnarvon, who was ten years older than she was. Albert de Rothschild brought wealth to the marriage after prolonged negotiations, paying off Carnarvon's debts of a staggering £150,000 and settling at least

£300,000 on the couple. These were enormous sums, so much so that one tart social commentator remarked that the Fifth Earl had married to "induce solvency." If this was a marriage entered into for love, it was also a remarkably successful business venture for the Fifth Earl. For the first time in years he was solvent and debt free. The marriage, on June 26, 1895, was a major social event of the London season.

Carnarvon's married life soon settled into a hectic routine of travel, lavish house parties, and the London season. Almina proved to be a remarkably adept hostess at Highclere and elsewhere. The Carnarvons entertained the Prince of Wales there in late 1895. The Earl imported 20,000 partridges from Hampshire for the occasion. The Prince and his companions shot about 11,000 of them.

Encounters with Egyptology

Porchy had first visited Egypt five years before his marriage and thoroughly enjoyed himself. The warm, dry climate suited his weak lungs. Damp, gray English winters brought on bronchitis and congested lungs that confined him to bed for weeks. Like Theodore Davis, he came to the Nile for his health and soon became an habitué. Physicians routinely advised their more affluent patients with lung problems to spend their winters along the Nile, so much so that Egypt had become a fashionable winter destination. The Carnarvons were there in 1902, but back in England for the summer racing, a passion shared by both Porchy and Almina. The same year saw Carnarvon founding the Highclere stud. He was a discerning judge of horseflesh or took sound advice. His gains in his first year from eleven winners was over £5,000.

He also developed a serious interest in "automobilism," to the point that he earned the nickname "Motor Carnarvon." He bought several of the earliest cars imported into Britain, the choice of British cars being very limited at the time. At one point, he owned a left-hand drive French Panhard Levassor, which had four gears and traveled at 13 miles an hour in top gear, a forerunner of today's automobiles in an era of ardent innovation. He became friends with a fellow Etonian, C. S. Rolls of Rolls Royce fame, who first went into business selling cars before building them. Carnavon was to own a series of quite powerful cars, being fined with regularity for speeding at more than 12 miles an hour while driving with goggles and a long, white coat. As we shall see, his passion for motorcars almost killed him.

In January 1903, the Carnarvons traveled to North America allegedly for a rest but actually for pure amusement that included a buffalo hunt in the Rockies and, of course, horse racing. In San Francisco's Bohemian Club, they had a chance encounter with Jeremiah Lynch, a former senator and gold prospector, who had traveled to Egypt and brought back a mummy with him that stood at the foot of the club staircase. He had also written *Egyptian Sketches*, a volume describing his travels that is, to put it mildly, a dull read.[7] Carnarvon had long had a casual interest in Egyptian antiquities, as had his father. Lynch entranced him with his stories of the tombs and mummies at

Deir el-Bahri on the west bank of the Nile opposite Luxor. This meeting may have triggered a much more serious interest in Egyptology for Carnarvon, perhaps beyond that of merely being a wealthy collector. The next year, he was again in Egypt and made enquiries about digging concessions. He was planning a hunting trip to India afterward but was forced to postpone it because of ill health. So he stayed in England and devoted most of his time to the turf.

Egypt was an appealing panacea for an aristocratic couple with health issues. After their marriage, the debonair Carnarvon and the Countess Almina became familiar figures during the winter season. The country was stable on the whole, under British control with a nominal Egyptian Khedive as statutory ruler. During his visits, the Earl had developed an interest in ancient art and photography. But by 1905 he was bored, tired of mindless balls and the protocols of formal costume and meaningless social maneuvering. Like other wealthy Nile visitors, he had sailed up the river by steamship or in a luxury *dahabeeyah* as far as the First Cataract at Aswan. The Carnarvons had visited the pyramids near Cairo, walked among the great columns of the Temples of Amun at Luxor and Karnak, and visited the Valley of the Kings. By chance, too, they'd been in Luxor when Theodore Davis had discovered Yuya and Tuya's sepulcher. Like many other notables, the Carnarvons had visited Davis's *Beduin* headquarters. Carnarvon knew that Davis was a serious antiquities collector. Perhaps this chance encounter, as well as the conversations with Jeremiah Lynch, prompted the Earl to consider digging himself.

With his far-flung social connections, Carnarvon had immediate access to Egypt's most powerful British officials. The real power lay in the hands of Lord Cromer, the Consul-General, a consummate imperial bureaucrat with close ties to Whitehall and the establishment.[8] He was an austere presence, who passed through Cairo's streets in an open carriage in formal dress, escorted by armed troopers, in a blatant display of British authority. A few distinguished visitors received an audience, among them Carnarvon, who shared his passion for shooting game birds. Cromer himself is said to have encouraged him to try archaeology as a way of passing time during his enforced winter exile. The Consul-General must have known that the Earl had a well-publicized reputation as a serious art collector dating back to his twenties. If Theodore Davis was digging up, and receiving, magnificent artifacts for his private collection, it would be logical to allow a well-connected English visitor with a cultivated eye and excellent taste a chance to do the same. Carnarvon seems to have embraced the idea with enthusiasm. Archaeology may have also appealed to his instincts as a sporting man accustomed to a risky flutter.

As mentioned, Lord Carnarvon had a long gambling history, dating back to when he was a teenager at Eton College. Diffident at dinner parties and on formal social occasions, the decisive, even authoritarian, side of his personality came to the fore when gambling was on the agenda. His marriage to Almina in 1895 brought Rothschild wealth to the family that had enabled him to finance his enthusiasms for horseflesh and automobiles. He was about to add a new, expensive pastime—archaeology. To Porchy, digging for the pharaohs began as a harmless pursuit, an entertaining and profitable way of passing time, and a gamble with ancient history. It was to become an obsession, ruled by the assertive side of his complex personality.

Seeking a Concession

The Carnarvons arrived in Cairo in early winter 1906, this time for a short visit. By then the fashionable season was in full swing, the city full of Thomas Cook's tourists on their way up the Nile in one of his steamships. Longer-term winter visitors crowded the better hotels, and there was, of course, the endless back-and-forth of British Raj officials pausing in Egypt before resuming their journey back home or to India. People like the Carnarvons stayed at Egypt's grandest caravanserai, Shepheard's Hotel. Familiar guests to the management, they moved into one of the hotel's luxurious suites, accompanied by mountains of luggage and their entourage of servants. Within days, the Earl secured an appointment with Lord Cromer at the imposing Agency building close to the Khedive's palace. He must have been well aware of Cromer's spare, and efficient, administrative methods. The Consul-General used a personalized system to govern the country, keeping the details in his head and working through a small group of trusted British officials. Carnarvon reminded his host about his suggestion of the year before. Cromer got right to the point.

"I've spoken to Garstin about a concession," he said. "He's in charge of antiquities. I've told him to give you one."

Carnarvon had met Sir William Garstin, Under Secretary of Public Works, on earlier occasions. One of Cromer's closest and most influential associates, Garstin was a brilliant irrigation engineer and a prominent member of the colonial establishment. He had overseen the construction of the Aswan Dam by the First Cataract in 1902 and revolutionized Egyptian agriculture in the process. He was well accustomed to dealing with aristocratic visitors. In all probability, the two men shared a drink on the Shepheard's Terrace, where much of Egypt's business came to pass in confidential discussions.

"Garstin, I want to dig near Luxor." The Fifth Earl sat in one of the much sought after rattan chairs on the terrace, his worn countenance, ravaged by high living and illness, wreathed in cigarette smoke. He expressed his wishes with the quiet assurance and sense of entitlement that went with his social standing. Across from him, the discreet, mustachioed Garstin sipped his drink and nodded. He was accustomed to such quiet approaches by the wealthy and well connected, which was the way much government business unfolded in an administration where everyone knew everyone else. As Carnarvon knew full well, his guest supervised the work of Gaston Maspero, the Director-General of Antiquities. Within a few days, Cromer and Garstin's "suggestions" had landed on Maspero's desk.

Figure 4.3 Shepheard's Hotel. *From American Colony (Jerusalem). Photo Dept., photographer, the G. Eric and Edith Matson Photograph Collection, courtesy of the Library of Congress.*

The portly, bearded Gaston Maspero presided over Egypt's archeological sites, whether royal burials, pyramids, temples, or humble worker's villages, with discreet authority. He was an elegant, urbane French Egyptologist of considerable reputation, who was an expert on tomb inscriptions, having deciphered hieroglyphs from an early age. Energetic and pragmatic, he had excavated Old Kingdom tombs and did a great deal to reorganize the Egyptian Museum in Cairo as well as establishing a network of local museums throughout the country. Like Garstin, he was well connected in the upper echelons of European society in Cairo. On paper, he wielded considerable authority, but he navigated a fine line that separated the needs of Egypt and its museums from the ambitions of the acquisitive overseas museums and wealthy sponsors who craved its antiquities. Amiable and adept in social situations, Maspero enjoyed good relations with both collectors and museum representatives in Europe and elsewhere. People liked him. He was also generous, perhaps over-generous, in allowing surplus finds over and above what he needed to leave the country. He is said to have told some of Theodore Davis's archaeologists to slip small artifacts and ornaments in their pockets and carry them out of the country without saying anything.

Like every senior civil servant, Maspero was well aware of the powerful connections and privileges enjoyed by wealthy aristocracy, the early twentieth-century equivalent of today's 1%. Fashionable Cairo was a small place, even at the height of the winter season, so he was acquainted with Carnarvon and his wife, even if the relationship was not a close one. Until he retired and left Egypt in 1914, Maspero seems to have liked Porchy and supported him without question. It was he who informed the inexperienced Earl that he would be granted a concession to excavate in the Theban Necropolis. Where among the tombs, he could not say, but he wrote to Arthur Weigall, his Antiquities Inspector at Luxor, instructing him to find a suitable site.

Arthur Weigall must have fumed when he received Maspero's instructions. Square-cut with prominent eyebrows, the young inspector—he was but 25 years old— was strong-minded and often outspoken. Despite his age, he had solid Egyptological qualifications and had worked at El-Amarna with Flinders Petrie. Above all he possessed a quality that Maspero valued—vast reservoirs of energy. He needed them, for the ravages of foreign excavators, tourists, and tomb robbers fed the insatiable antiquities markets of Europe and North America. He had learned a great deal about the ways of the wealthy from his dealings with the authoritarian Theodore Davis, who was accustomed to getting his way in the face of daunting obstacles. He had resolute views on the right ways to go about exploring disturbed, and undisturbed, tombs. It was not something that one left to wealthy gentlemen unless they had competent archaeologists with them. He once remarked in a letter to a colleague: "The records of the past are not ours to play with: in the manner of big game in Uganda, they should be disturbed only by those with a strictly worded license."[9] Now he was expected to provide yet another bored, but well connected, affluent gentleman with an archaeological site to amuse himself.

To give Carnarvon a concession in the Necropolis was an unusually bold decision by his superiors, a measure of the Earl's enormous social prestige, not his expertise. As Porchy himself admitted, he had no experience of excavation whatsoever, let alone of the often harsh conditions of Egyptian digging. Garstin and Maspero had given the Earl a free hand, the safeguard being Weigall's ability to steer him to an unproductive site where failure was almost guaranteed and he might lose interest in a few days. We don't know whether the inspector had met Carnarvon before, but he must have been both astonished and disconcerted to learn that the Earl planned to excavate without any previous experience and with no expert assistance whatsoever. He knew full well that he could not protest the decision, so he pondered his dilemma and looked across the Nile at the vast Theban Necropolis on the West Bank. It all came down to a simple question. Where would Carnarvon do the least damage?

Tutankhamun the Justified

"Year 12 . . . [The king and queen] appeared on the great carrying-chair of gold to receive the tribute of Kharu [Syria-Palestine] and Kush [Nubia], the West and East. All countries collected together at one time, and the lands in the midst of the sea, bringing offerings to the king upon the great throne of Akhet-Aten . . . Granting to them the breath of life."[1]

Long before Akhenaten and Tutankhamun's time, trading networks connected Mesopotamia with the Eastern Mediterranean, Anatolia (what is now Turkey), and Central Asia. Donkey caravans were the staples of overland trade, connecting the Tigris and Euphrates Valleys with coastal cities such as Byblos. By 1800 B.C., the Assyrians of present-day northern Iraq had established trading colonies in Anatolia, exchanging textiles and tin for gold. Semitic Akkadian, written in cuneiform, became the lingua franca of diplomacy, used by rulers and merchants from the Persian Gulf to the Nile. The Egyptians were important players in the polyglot maritime trade that linked the Nile and Levant with copper-rich Cyprus, the Aegean islands, and Greece.

These trading enterprises flourished against a volatile geopolitical backdrop. In the north, Hittite kings controlled much of Anatolia and northwestern Syria. Their foes, the Hurrians, a patchwork of kingdoms centered on Mitanni, presided over the Upper Euphrates and northeastern Syria. To the east lay another aggressive presence, the Assyrians and Babylonia. Then there were the pharaohs, who had major economic interests in the Levant, which they controlled through a maze of vassal rulers. By Thutmosis IV's time in the early fourteenth century B.C., Amurru, a former Egyptian ally, had risen to prominence and changed its allegiance to the Hittites. For a time, however, Egypt's client states kept the eastern frontiers secure, which accounted for Akhenaten's Presentation of Inu (Tribute) and its lavish offerings.

Egypt remained the dominant power in the checkerboard of rivalries across the eastern Mediterranean in Akhenaten's time, whence the elaborate Presentation of

Inu convened in Year 12 of the pharaoh's reign. We know of the event from scenes on the walls of the tombs of two high officials—Huya, the steward of Queen Tiye, Amenhotep II's widow, and the royal scribe Merye, High Priest of Aten, who was buried next to her at Akhetaten. Sitting in state, Akhenaten received manufactured and raw materials from throughout his realm, as well as bound prisoners that included both Nubians and Hittites.

Life! Prosperity! Health!

Tutankhaten was born in Year 1 or Year 2, so he was still very young when the great diplomatic gathering brought gifts from much of the known world. Being the heir, he would have appeared regularly at ceremonies of all kinds, standing quietly among the high officials and courtiers who attended the pharaoh and his queen on formal occasions. An embroidered tunic worn by Tutankhaten as a child at a formal ceremony came from his tomb, adorned with embroidered rosettes and hieroglyphic signs associated with the heb-sed ceremony.[2] His tutor, Sennedjem, would have been by his side, whispering in the prince's ear if he fidgeted or failed to pay attention. What pharaohs wore in daily life is somewhat of a mystery. Judging from the boy king's sepulcher, he sometimes wore cloaks, robes, and knee-length tunics, also woven sashes, which were long enough to go several times around the waist, a garment typical of royalty and, less elaborately, of nobles. On official occasions, the pharaoh wore several forms of crown, fine pectorals, a kilt, sandals, and a bull's tail, an ancient symbol of Egyptian kingship. His jewelry was exquisite, carefully stored in his tomb: pectorals, bracelets, amulets, earrings, bracelets, and rings, many with symbolic motifs. Except on formal occasions,[3] much of the time, Tutankhaten probably dressed like others—in kilts, tunics, and loincloths, but always made of the finest linen and other carefully selected raw materials.

Etiquette and rigid protocol surrounded Akhenaten's daily routine and required the services of officials to oversee them. We have none of the details but can glean something from earlier and later accounts of other pharaohs. There were functionaries who presided over the ruler's bathing and grooming, including his shaving, which included his head, so he typically wore a wig. The same was true of his successor. Tutankhamun's tomb contains a white box with his shaving equipment: "The equipment of His Majesty Life! Prosperity! Health!" Like Akhenaten, Tutankhamun's skin was moisturized with pure oils and fats; kohl, made from galena, adorned his eyes. Tutankhamun's cosmetics duly appear in his tombs, including kohl sticks and ointment container, also mirror cases.

Meanwhile, the prince's education never ceased. As he grew older, Tutankhaten continued to learn the principles of royal leadership, completed ever more elaborate writing exercises on gesso-covered wooden tablets, and studied mathematics. Like other princes, he led a life of learning, relaxation, and sport, hunting in the desert and marshes and playing board games such as senet.

Figure 5.1 *Senet* table. © *Griffith Institute, University of Oxford.*

Senet was already an ancient game in Tutankhaten's time, played with pieces on a board of squares, somewhat like backgammon. People were playing it as early as 3100 B.C., but by Akhenaten's time it had become far more than a casual pastime. Now it was a talisman for the journey of the dead, who played the game against Fate. An elegant senet game box on a sled with feline legs came from the cramped annex in Tutankhaten's tomb (for tomb plan, see chapter 10). The upper and lower surfaces of the box are veneered with ivory, with raised strips dividing the surface into thirty squares. Senet players moved their ivory or gold pieces according to the casts of knucklebones or casting sticks, several of which also were in the sepulcher. Quite apart from the pleasure of winning, successful players were considered to be under the protection of the major gods, which is why the game appears in noble and royal tombs. A total of four senet sets came from the sepulcher, one of them a portable one with a carving of the pharoah and Amnkhesenamun on one end. Perhaps they played the game together.

Any form of physical activity must have challenged the young prince with his deformed foot. He may have used a stick on a daily basis and was of slender build, which must have made it hard for him to draw a bow or cast a spear, both basic military skills inculcated into a future king who would lead, at least symbolically, his armies into battle. Judging from inscriptions from earlier reigns, royal tutors would have taught him to use a bow and arrow, also the basic arts of war. When he finally became a teenager, the young prince, now pharaoh, may have ridden donkeys and horses and hunted small animals—pastimes that would have removed him briefly from the stiff formality of the court—but always under the watchful eye of royal guards. He would also have learned how to ride a chariot.

"He Who Appears on His Team of Horses"

"Hold on to the rail." "Balance yourself," "Put your feet apart." The commands from the prince's chariot master rang loud across the military parade ground. Feverishly, Tutankhaten clung to the car, frightened, apprehensive. The chariot master urged the horses into a walk, then a trot. The tense prince closed his eyes, then opened them. He relaxed as the chariot gathered speed, for the ride was more comfortable than he had expected. A touch of the whip, the horses broke into a headlong gallop, then slowed for a sharp turn. The chariot master drove round and round the parade ground, always with a sharp eye on his passenger. Fine dust settled on Tutankhaten's now animated face. He felt an unfamiliar freedom, a distance from the sterile protocol of the palace, and itched to handle the reins. The chariot master suddenly headed out of the dusty arena into open desert. As he accelerated, the car jounced and bumped over the uneven ground. "Relax," growled the charioteer. "You are quite safe." Tutankhaten nodded and smiled, now much more at ease. Back on the parade ground, the chariot slowed. The chariot master handed his charge the reins as the horses slowed to a walk, showed him how to wrap them around his waist, how to steer the chariot left and right. "Good," said the driver. "You will become a skilled driver." As Tutankhaten lowered himself carefully from the car, the tutor Sennedjem nodded to the chariot master in approval. Here was something at which the young prince could excel.

A hypothetical scenario, of course, but there's no question that chariots were important in Tutankhaten's life. No less than six of them came from his sepulcher.[4] The pharaoh's armies were mainly foot soldiers, armed with spears or swords and large leather shields. Others trained as archers, but the elite were the charioteers, who formed a separate component of the army, deployed in formation, wearing leather tunics and bronze helmets. Every pharaoh and royal prince aspired to be part of this prestigious unit. Chariots rode along the enemy lines firing arrows. They never charged their foes directly. They were formidable weapons, introduced to the Nile Valley by Semitic Hyksos chiefs from the Levant some generations earlier, then refined by Egyptian artisans. The flat plains of the Delta and arid desert terrain made this horse-drawn weaponry a formidable part of the military arsenal, which assumed great symbolic importance as a token of pharaonic power and victory. It was no coincidence that a wooden box in Tutankhaten's tomb depicted him alone in a chariot conquering his Asian and Nubian foes. The lid shows him hunting lions and other prey in the desert.

The six chariots from the future pharaoh's sepulcher show just how skillfully

Figure 5.2   Tutankhamun's ceremonial chariot. © *Griffith Institute, University of Oxford.*

Egyptian woodworkers had improved on the original Asian design. Two of the chariots were large ceremonial vehicles, covered with gesso, gold, and inlaid with glass and ivory. With their gold-leaf covered wheels, they may never have been ridden, perhaps were built just for the tomb. Another smaller one was highly decorated, presumably, like the larger ones, for processional use. Then there were three lighter hunting chariots that the king could have used on a daily basis. They are simple and elegant, with six-spoked wheels made of an elastic timber fitted with flexible wood rim "tires." The combination of relatively flexible wheels and the tires absorbed bumps very effectively, much in the same way as today's independent suspension on automobiles. The axle bearings, lubricated with animal grease, brought a hard material against a soft one. These were fast, thoroughbred chariots that could be driven at speeds up to 25 mph or more over irregular surfaces and hard sand dunes. Interlaced leather thongs formed the floor of the car, covered with an animal skin or a linen rug with a long pile. The elasticity of the floor absorbed bumps, helped by the wheels being set far back and the springiness of the center pole. Everything was bound together with leather or hide lashings, which gave the chariot an unusual flexibility. These were sophisticated vehicles that were comfortable to ride fast, which made them ideal for hunting in the desert at the edge of the Nile Valley—and easy for a frail prince to drive.

Egyptian chariots were narrow, usually large enough to carry only two people standing upright. The horses that drew them were carefully paired, often adorned with feathers, and capable of hauling the chariots at high speed. The driver served as the archer, his companion bearing a shield to protect him. Each chariot had its own runner,

Figure 5.3   Tutankhamun hunting waterfowl. *Kenneth Garrett/National Geographic Creative.*

who defended the horses with a javelin. Pharaohs were usually depicted riding alone, the harness warped around their waists, but this was symbolic fiction. The driver used a short whip. Several whip stocks (handles) came from the king's sepulcher, one of them bearing the pharaoh's titles: "he who appears upon his team of horses as when Re ascends." Another one may have belonged to a princely horse master.

As part of his training, Tutankhaten would have been taught how to drive and how to shoot arrows from a moving chariot. He was also an enthusiastic hunter. A golden fan trimmed with alternating brown and white ostrich feathers found between the third and fourth shrines in the burial chamber shows Tutankhamun in a chariot shooting ostriches in the desert near Memphis, striking two of them with arrows. His hunting dog moves in to collect the prey. Stone blocks from Karnak depict the king hunting lions and bulls. We can imagine him shooting at targets, then, after some months, riding into the desert in search of gazelle and other game. If he went after more formidable game as a boy, the beasts were probably corralled before he rode out. Tutankhaten would have never been alone. Some other chariots would always be close by, ready to protect the prince in case of an ambush. With his frail build and deformed leg, Tutankhaten may have had some trouble balancing in the chariot and mustering the strength to pull a bow. But he must have had some success, for archery equipment lay throughout his tomb, including both elaborately decorated composite bows and simpler weapons, as well as reed arrows. One statue of the pharaoh in the tomb shows him standing on a papyrus reed canoe as if he speared fish in the reeds. Numerous throwing sticks attest to bird hunting, probably in the marshes. A scene on a golden shrine in the antechamber shows the pharaoh seated hunting wildfowl with a bow. His wife hands him arrows as he opens fire. A favorite place for marsh hunting would have been the Fayum Depression in the desert west of the Nile.

Diplomacy

Archery and chariot driving were one thing, but preparation for the throne was the overwhelming priority. Tutankhaten would have spent much of his time at banquets and formal affairs of state, which must have been an ordeal for an adolescent. Like other prospective pharaohs, he would have learned the most secret and profound rituals of the state religion, in his case of Aten, as well as cosmology. Under normal circumstances, he would have become a reasonably high official in his late teens, perhaps an overseer of cattle for a temple or a high priest. Even when approaching his teenage years, he was present at the center of Egyptian affairs under a pharaoh whose primary obsession was Aten and religious faith. Akhenaten followed a common precedent and appointed a coregent, perhaps at first Nefertiti, who may have died in 1337 B.C., year thirteen of Akhenaten's reign. A short time later, a little known royal, Ankhkheperure Smenkhkare, probably Tutankhaten's half-brother from a lesser wife, became regent, then king.

The pharaoh could never forget that he presided over a vast, increasingly diverse, and often restless, state that was at uneasy peace with its neighbors and sometimes at war with them. The young prince spent his early teenage years surrounded by high officials and hearing at least the gossip that surrounded the state's dealings with other monarchs across the eastern Mediterranean world. As far as we can tell, Akhenaten's reign was peaceful, except for one possible attack on Kadesh in northern Syria late in his reign, but the records are sketchy at best.

Fortunately, two sets of cuneiform tablets throw light on the complex relationships between Egypt and other states. One collection, found at Amarna in 1887, documents correspondence between various rulers and Amenhotep III, Akhenaten, and Tutankhamun.[5] A second group of tablets come from the Hittite archives at Boghazkoy in Anatolia. These focus in particular on the deeds of a powerful Hittite king, Shuppiluliumash I, who came to power shortly before Akhenaten became pharaoh. This aggressive monarch had ambitious expansion plans. He conquered an Egyptian ally, Mitanni, and tussled with Egypt over some of its client states and cities, including Kadesh. At this point, the Hittites did not directly attack Egyptian possessions, but they seized control of allied city-states in northern Syria in what one observer has aptly called a form of "cold war." Threatened allies wrote to the pharaoh asking for assistance, but apparently to no avail, as Hittite incursions continued. This was the complex diplomatic and potentially military situation that Tutankhaten inherited as pharaoh.

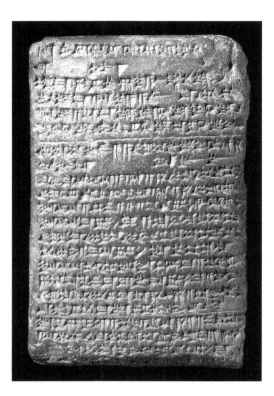

Formality and Routine

For all the seeming informality of his family life depicted on temple walls, Akhenaten lived a rigorously scheduled life, which extended far beyond his waking routine and meals. Greek historian Diodorus Siculus wrote of the pharaoh in the first century B.C. that "there was a set time not only for his holding audiences or rendering judgments, but even for his taking a walk, bathing, and sleeping with his wife, and in a word for every act of his life."[6] The formality may have varied, but it was always there. So were the constant streams of letters and dispatches that reached the pharaoh every morning. New Kingdom texts from high officials' tombs record that the vizier met with the king early in the day, either alone or with other senior officials, both to make obeisance and also to brief him on current issues. They might give advice, but the pharaoh, and only the pharaoh, made the decisions.

As he grew older, Tutankhamun would have been present at some of these sessions, as he would have been at major religious ceremonies, and sometimes when the king acted as a judge. He acquired at least a basic knowledge of a position that set him at the pinnacle of a complete bureaucracy of state with three branches—administrative, military, and religious. He had to be literate in each but had to rely heavily on the advice given by his senior, most trusted officials. These were the individuals who actually ran the state, their influence depending on the ability of, and power wielded by, the ruler. In the case of Akhenaten, who was obsessed with the Aten, it is likely that his most senior officials had considerable freedom of action. The pharaoh had surrounded himself, as all Egyptian kings did, with courtiers and officials who were loyal to him. In Akhenaten's case, this would have meant individuals with a profound belief in the Aten. The veneer of religious conformity soon dissolved after Tutankhaten came to the throne.

For all his secular worries, especially diplomacy and taxation, Akhenaten lived out his reign governed largely by a daily routine of ritual and religious practice. He relied heavily on a handful of senior officials, notable among them his chief adviser, Ay, who was to play a decisive role in Tutankhaten's life. He was the pharaoh's right-hand man, even more so than the king's two viziers, who presided over Lower and Upper Egypt.

Ay, God's Father

Ay-It-Netjar ("Ay, Father of the Gods") was born in Ipu (modern-day Akmim) in Upper Egypt.[7] In Ancient Egyptian times, it was an important place, the capital of the ninth nome (province) of the country. Akmim was perhaps the birthplace of Yuya, a senior chariotry officer under Amenhotep III, whose tomb Theodore Davis opened in 1905. Ay may have been one of his sons, a brother of Tiye, who became the Great Wife of Amenhotep III. This family connection gave him status in the pharaoh's court, where there was already an unusual devotion to Aten. Ay seems to have embraced the cult with what may have been calculated enthusiasm, for he achieved prominence at Akhenaten's court. Whether his devotion to Aten was a matter of conviction or convenience is intriguing, given what happened when the pharaoh died. He was on the military side, at first a troop commander, then an Overseer of Horses before coming Overseer of All the Horses of His Majesty, a title found in a tomb for him excavated during Akhenaten's reign. Titles were important measures of status in the pharaoh's court, and Ay does not disappoint. As was Count Sennerdjem, he was a Fan-Bearer on the Right Side of the King. Since he may have been Nefertiti's father, the titles are hardly surprising.

Ay would have been an imposing figure at court, giving advice, providing information, and carrying out the pharaoh's orders. The Akhetaten-based sculptor Thutmose, who called himself Chief of Works and owned the workshop where the famous painted portrait of Queen Nefertiti came to light, executed a portrait said to be that of the vizier.[8] He stares into the distance with closed, full lips, giving an impression of complete assurance, even arrogance. This was a formidable man with a strong personality, with ties to the military elite—the chariotry. People often refer to him as the vizier, but this may not have been the case. In fact, it does not really matter, because of Ay's impeccable connections to the royal family. He had the ear of Akhenaten and was constantly at his side. Ay was the most important person at court and, for that matter, in the kingdom as well. Politically adept, close to the throne, and involved in most of the great affairs of state, Ay was a powerful presence in a palace that teemed with factions and rivalries, probably even more than usual because of Akhenaten's religious beliefs, which had deeply offended the traditionalist followers of the sun god Amun.

One question must have preoccupied those who surrounded the pharaoh. Who was to succeed Akhenaten if he died suddenly, or plague felled members of the court, including the king? Ay must have calculated the odds and made sure that the young and frail Tutankhaten valued his advice. He stayed close to the pharaoh-to-be, offering advice, imparting wisdom and precedent, rebuking him strongly and with a freedom that would be unthinkable when Tutankhaten became king. This hard, calculating, and shrewd man must have been a longer-term thinker than many at the court. He grappled with potential problems of a regency should the pharaoh die soon and, knowing the heir's fragile health, must have calculated who would succeed him if he died childless. Tutankhaten must have spent much time in Ay's company, both on formal occasions and as part of his schooling. Ay and the prince's tutor, Count Sennedjem, kept careful track of the young man, as he studied for the kingship in the shadows of Akhenaten, the living god, Effective for the Aten.

Tutankhaten Becomes Pharaoh

Akhenaten's reign lasted seventeen years, five of them as Amenhotep IV, the remainder as Akhenaten, when he abandoned Egypt's traditional deities. He died in either 1336 or 1334 B.C., when Tutankhaten was eight or nine years old. The cause of his death is unknown, but it may have been sudden, perhaps even as a result of plague, which was commonplace along the Nile during the New Kingdom. The court was plunged into mourning. The mummified king was buried in a rock-cut tomb in the eastern mountains above Akhetaten.

At this moment, Tutankhaten's life changed profoundly. He now became high priest and a living god, the intermediary between the living and the supernatural. This scrawny young man now became the ancient symbol of *ma'at*, order and equilibrium, the central tenet of Egyptian life. He was now the ultimate authority, the decision maker, the symbolic leader of men in battle. He changed, apparently suddenly, from being a preteenager to a pharaoh. Clearly, however, he was too young to assume the throne, so the question of a regency plunged the country into uncertainty.

Decisive steps were needed to ensure continuity at a time of considerable social unrest. Quite what happened next has engaged scholars for more than a century. One can but navigate between the hazardous shoals of academic controversy, with no signs of resolution in sight.[9] Distilling a complex detective story into a plausible scenario, one may suggest that the players beyond the young pharaoh himself were Queen Nefertiti, who had exercised considerable power during her husband's reign and before her death, two mysterious individuals—a woman named Neferneferuaten and a man, Ankhkheperure Smenkhkare—and, undoubtedly in the background, Ay. Was there a coregency, Neferneferuaten being Nefertiti, or one of Akhenaten, or were there two reigns, one by Neferneferuaten, the other by Smenkhkare? Or were the two the same person but with different names? If there were two reigns, they were short ones. Of the two, a brief two- or three-year reign by Smenkhkare seems most likely. Since the records of the Amarna pharaohs, including Tutankhamun, were destroyed by his successor, we have little to go on, and it's best to admit that we simply don't know. All that is certain is that Tutankhamun assumed the reins of power and that Ay was literally the king's shadow, to the point that he is seen occupying a chariot with him.

Tutankhaten ascended to the throne with a very narrow view of the world, and indeed of his own kingdom. He was literate, had an intense training in ritual and in Aten's cosmology but little or no practical experience of wider affairs. He had friends among young princes and nobles at the court, but a huge social gulf separated him from them, defined by centuries of formality and protocol. He knew no commoners except his servants and those who maintained and guarded palaces and the temples. How much he traveled beyond the confines of Akhentaten is unknown, but he must have accompanied his father on some of his formal progresses up and down the Nile in the royal barge. The new king's knowledge of diplomacy and warfare came from high officials such as Ay and senior generals, among them a relative newcomer to the court, a military man named Horemheb, whom we shall encounter in Chapter 7. As Tutankhaten settled in as pharaoh, he found himself hemmed in by these two powerful advisers, both ambitious and ruthless men, who exercised a powerful influence on his decisions from day one of his reign.

She Who Lives through the Aten

One immediate issue came to the fore—the matter of the succession. At issue here was the family line, the continuity of the dynasty. To avoid succession disputes, the eighteenth-Dynasty pharaohs encouraged intermarriage between members of the royal family. In Tutankhamun's case, there may have been a problem of dynastic legitimacy, traditionally solved by marrying princes to their half-sisters, whose parents were the pharaoh and the Great Royal Wife. The problem was particularly acute when Tutankhaten came to the throne, for the future of the Aten cult was at stake. A royal marriage was now a matter of urgency to ensure continued religious purity, especially when the heir was of poor health. Clearly, he should marry just as soon as possible.

Royal marriages were arranged, as they usually were for monarchs in ancient

Figure 5.5 Tutankhamun and Ankhesenamun depicted on the back of a throne in the pharaoh's tomb. © *Sandro Vannini/Corbis*.

times. The new pharaoh's chosen wife was Ankhesenpaaten ("She Who Lives through the Aten"), the third daughter of Akhenaten and Nefertiti, probably a couple of years older than the king and perhaps his half-sister.* Little is known about her, but she was probably Ay's granddaughter and was apparently previously married for short periods both to her father, perhaps only symbolically as Great Wife, and to Smenkhkare.[10] The couple had grown up together and knew each other well. Both the new queen's previous unions were, of course, marriages only in name, as was her relationship with the new pharaoh until they both reached puberty and could consummate their relationship. Whether it was a love match we will never know, but the pictures of them are carefully choreographed to show affection. We know nothing of their relationship except for symbolized depictions, but they may have been devoted to one another. In a famous scene on the back of a golden throne from the antechamber, Tutankhamun sits on a throne in a garden, while Ankhesenamun anoints his shoulder with perfumed ointment; the rays of the Aten descend on the couple—perhaps the throne was a relic from Akhetaten days. Both Aten and Amun's names appear, as if the throne had been reworked.

*Like Tutankhamun, her name was changed during the early years of the young pharaoh's reign to Ankhesenamun ("She Who Lives through Amun").

Over the next decade, Ankhesenamun gave birth to two daughters, both of whom were stillborn. Both were buried in the king's sepulcher. There are hints that the pharaoh may have had other children who lived, perhaps from another wife, but there is no definite record of them.

The power behind the regency and the throne was Ay, so well connected to the royal family and to Tutankhaten that he was immune from intrigue. The failure of the royal couple to produce an heir must have fueled Ay's already powerful ambition to take over the throne one day. In the meantime, he molded and shaped the pharaoh's thinking during a critical, and potentially very dangerous, period, when bold decisions in the royal name would have been far beyond the capability of a king barely entering his second decade.

The changes seem to have begun almost at once. Tutankhaten's coronation took place not at Akhentaten but at Memphis in Lower Egypt, the traditional royal capital. His name changed almost at once to Nebkheperure Tutankhamun ("Living Image of Amun").* On the appointed day, the new pharaoh assumed the Double Crown of Upper and Lower Egypt, the symbol of his rule over the Two Lands.[11] He would have knelt before Amun, received his crook and flail (a child-sized example was in his tomb, also a larger set that he used as he grew up), symbols of his power, and performed a series of rituals that proclaimed him as the legitimate ruler, ratified and blessed by the gods. The coronation would have ended with an elaborate parade with the bejeweled pharaoh wearing a crown and carrying his flail and crook appearing among the people. *Ma'at* was restored. Symbolic order once again descended on the kingdom.

If Tutankhamun indeed went through the traditional ceremony, and there is every reason to belief that he did, it would have been a striking break from the doctrines of the Aten. That his coronation was at Memphis was a powerful symbolic gesture that life was not the same. Ay and his fellow officials seem to have cast off the fetters of Aten in short order. From the beginning of his reign, Tutankhamun ruled from Memphis. His court never assembled at Akhentaten, even if the administrative machinery there continued on an increasingly smaller scale, to be snuffed out entirely by the third or fourth year of the new reign.

Tutankhamun presided over a state that was casting off the shackles of Aten, the Sun Disk. As the old order kicked into gear once more, the center of religious gravity shifted from Akhenaten's now abandoned capital back to Karnak and Luxor. Not that the young pharaoh had much to do with all this himself. He was a puppet in the hands of powerful officials, principal among them Ay and a new and increasingly important player, General Horemheb.

*From here on, I refer to the pharaoh as Tutankhamun.

"The Records of the Past Are Not Ours to Play With"

The Theban Necropolis, December 1907. Carnarvon lounged in a comfortable chair inside his tent, wreathed in cigarette smoke. More than a hundred chattering workers and basket boys labored in the rubble close downwind. Basketful after basketful of boulders slid down the nearby hillside. A thin cloak of dust hovered inside the spacious tent, but at least the netting kept the flies at bay. The Earl was alone, dressed in a brown three-piece suit, gold watch chain across the waistcoat. A woolen cardigan worn under his vest protected him against the chilly north wind. Because of his fragile health, he felt the cold more than most people. A white-clad servant stood behind him, coffee pot close at hand.

The work slowed as a donkey approached from the nearby village. The *reises* (foremen) shouted at the men, but they ignored them. A compact, well-dressed Englishman dismounted by the tent and handed the reins to Carnarvon's servant. The Earl pushed aside the netting. A warm smile twitched under his mustache. "Ah, Weigall," he said. "I was wondering when you'd turn up."

Weigall and Carnarvon

The hubbub of the dig resumed. Arthur Weigall was well known in the local villages. The young Chief Inspector of Antiquities for Upper Egypt was a frequent visitor, often accompanied by distinguished visitors touring the nearby Valley of the Kings. He was more than familiar with wealthy, often demanding visitors intoxicated by the lure of gold-adorned royal burials, but he liked Carnarvon. "A good sort," he wrote when reporting on the excavations to Egyptologist Francis Griffith.

"What have you found?" asked Weigall as he sipped coffee and puffed on the cigar that was never far from his lips.

"Nothing except the stuff in the basket," Carnarvon replied, lighting a cigarette in his trademark golden holder. He gestured to a large basket near the entrance. "And that's of no importance."

Weigall sifted through the mélange of potsherds, mummy fragments, and broken human bones. "Just as I'd expected," he thought to himself. He had assigned Carnarvon a well worked over location, assuming he would soon give up.

"You're right," he replied, expecting the Earl to be discouraged, "Aren't you bored?"

Carnarvon was a reserved man, from an aristocratic culture that shunned emotion in public. But his eyes lit up with enthusiasm.

"Bored? Quite the contrary. This is far more exciting than sitting in the Winter Palace making polite conversation to fashionable invalids. Besides, all this fresh air is good for me. I haven't felt so good in weeks. Just watching the dig and being in the open air makes me feel a new man."

"But aren't you discouraged by the lack of finds after the tomb pit you found a couple of weeks ago turned out to be empty?" The emerging pit had caused a brief frisson of excitement in the Antiquities Department, which soon dispersed when there was nothing inside.

"Three weeks more of digging left," replied the Earl. "That's nothing, and there's always a chance we'll find something important. Besides, there's other places to search." He pointed to various spots, chosen at random on the advice of his workers because they looked promising. I've just started." A cloud of dust caused him to sneeze. "This is like horseracing—a gamble with high stakes."

Weigall was well aware that the Earl's notion of an archaeological gamble was a search for undisturbed pharaohs in the nearby Valley of the Kings.[1] He thanked his lucky stars that the American millionaire Theodore Davis was in firm possession of the most valuable concession along the Nile. At least he had the sense to leave the work to an experienced excavator. Archaeology was not a sport but something to be undertaken with scientific respect. With luck, he'd be rid of the Earl at the end of the season.

A shout came from the nearby excavation. A *reis* beckoned; the workers leaned on their picks; an unwonted silence descended on the diggings. Carnarvon and Weigall put on their headgear, in the Earl's case his trademark hat with a white band. As inspector, Weigall wore that token of European authority—a solar pith helmet. With deliberate calm, they made their way toward a cavity in the rubble. Weigall gestured for a hand brush. As he reached for it, the Earl took it from him. He knelt down and peered at a just exposed black object. His brush strokes caressed the sides of the find, a large cat figure with yellow eyes that glared at the intruders. Gravel and sand fell away with each brush stroke. A circle of intent faces surrounded the Earl, muttering to one another. Working from either side, Carnarvon and Weigall lifted the pitch-covered wooden mummy case with care and placed it on the side of the trench. The cat's sinister eyes stared at everybody as they clustered around to admire the find. The *reis* shouted at the men to resume work. With infinite care, Carnarvon carried his trophy to the tent.

Weigall examined the cat with expert hands. "It's a wooden mummy case. There's a bandaged cat inside."

"My first important find!" cried the Earl, ignoring the fact that thousands of mummified cats had come from cemeteries up and down the Nile. "I wonder what we'll find next!"

Weigall said nothing, but he had seen the excited light in the Earl's eyes. As he accompanied Carnarvon and the cat across the river, so the Earl could show it off to Almina and his friends in the refined comfort of the Winter Palace Hotel in Luxor, he pondered Carnarvon's moment of truth. Carnarvon had realized that archaeology was far more than a game.

The Theban Necropolis

Carnarvon's concession assigned him a well worked over sector of one of the largest and most complex archaeological locations in the world. One could call the necropolis a site, but that would be technically inaccurate. Hundreds of graves, abandoned villages, mortuary temples, and other remains cluttered the vast necropolis, which had been a "city of the dead" for thousands of years. The tombs and temples on the west bank had attracted tomb robbers and treasure hunters since the time of the pharaohs. Harsh penalties, even death, had not deterred them, for untold riches lay beneath their feet. Roman tourists fossicked here; so did General Napoléon's soldiers and his learned savants in 1798. In those days, rich harvests of antiquities lay in tomb and sepulcher for the gathering. Giovanni Belzoni had found the Temples of Amun at Luxor and Karnak overrun with the minions of his rival the French consul Bernardino Drovetti, in 1817. Drovetti's ruffians were notorious for their violence. They resented any outsider who impinged on their self-proclaimed archaeological monopoly. So Belzoni retreated to the west bank and befriended the villagers of Qurna, whose inhabitants had been inveterate tomb robbers for centuries. They were, he wrote, "superior to any other Arabs in cunning and deceit," useful qualifications for their profession.[2] The necropolis and nearby hills were an endless source of mummies and papyri sold to tourists for high prices. He remarked that the Qurnese preferred tomb robbing to agriculture. They lived in nearby caves and abandoned tombs, among "hands, feet, and sculls."

One cannot blame the Qurnese for turning to tomb robbing when potential profit lay on every side. The Theban Necropolis extended about 8 kilometers (5 miles) along the west bank of the Nile opposite Luxor. Thousands of Ancient Egyptians lay there, some dating to earlier than 2500 B.C., the latest buried in Ptolemaic times about 2,000 years ago. Burials, mostly placed in reused older tombs, continued deep into Roman times. High officials and their wives occupied painted and furnished tombs; artisans lay in well-appointed sepulchers; the mummified remains of anonymous common folk lay stacked in narrow defiles in the cliffs. By Carnarvon's time, the vast cemetery was a confused, light-brown wilderness of rubble and debris left by frustrated excavators. Heaps of ancient and modern garbage, shreds of linen mummy wrappings, fragments of coffins, and thousands of potsherds protruded from the sand. To find anything required moving jumbled accumulations of rocky debris and spoil heaps left by earlier excavators. A confusion of shattered mortuary chapels and temples lay on every side. The British and French authorities had done much to curtail illegal digging by 1907. Nevertheless, they granted concessions that saw wealthy visitors and their hired archaeologists attacking the rubble of the necropolis with hundreds of workers, in most cases without success.

An occasional spectacular discovery hit the headlines. In 1906, the Italian Egyptologist Professor Ernesto Schiaparelli had labored with 250 workers for some months before locating the tomb of the royal architect Kha and his wife Merit.[3] Weigall was at his side when the Italian opened the undisturbed sepulcher of this high Theban official of the fourteenth century B.C. The tomb contained the nested coffins and lavish supplies of food, clothing, and other possessions for eternity. With finds like this, and those of Theodore Davis, in the headlines, one cannot blame the bored and acquisitive Carnarvon for his interest in a concession. Weigall assumed that like other affluent excavators he would move from place to place in search of he called the "plums." In reality, excavation in the necropolis was a dreary, unspectacular business that involved moving tons of rubble and sand without finding anything.

One can read the thoughts that passed through Weigall's expert and cynical mind. He assumed that Carnarvon was very casual about archaeology, gambling on rich finds, assuming they would come to hand, digging being somewhat akin to a game of tennis or bird hunting. It was a matter of bagging the game. The young inspector balanced the interests of the government against those of a rank amateur. After careful thought, he assigned the Earl a location on a plateau known as Sheikh Abdel Gurna close to the tomb robbers' village. Carnarvon himself always admitted that he knew nothing about excavation, let alone Egyptology. No fool, and too well-mannered to say so, he assumed that he had been allotted the site to keep him out of mischief, which was, in fact, the truth.

Traveling to Luxor

When Porchy and Almina traveled from Cairo to Luxor in November 1907, Carnarvon exuded a novice gambler's confidence. For centuries, tourists had traveled upriver in *dahabiyyahs*, luxurious riverboats propelled by sails, the current, and towed by the crew.[4] A typical excursion to the First Cataract and back from Cairo would take about two months. Then came steamships and the energetic Thomas Cook, who organized

Figure 6.1 Lord Carnarvon reading in Howard Carter's house; reading was one of his addictions.
© *Griffith Institute, University of Oxford.*

his first excursion to Egypt in 1869. By the early years of the twentieth century, the company ran three grades of steamship on the river, which made the circuit between Cairo and Aswan every two weeks during the winter season. The trip lasted some three weeks, the comforts depending on the affluence of the passengers. The trips were organized according to careful schedules, but the disadvantage for people like the elitist Carnarvons was the somewhat diverse multinational society aboard. Discerning passengers chose cabin companions with care. Cook also offered luxury *dahabiyyahs* designed for passengers desiring absolute privacy. They had no prearranged schedule and stopped wherever the clients wished. Some steam-powered examples were side-wheelers; one of them, the *Jonas*, had nine luxury cabins with river views from the portholes and a main saloon on the upper deck. There was electric light and two bathrooms for the eleven passengers. *Jonas* was expensive—$2,000 for a month for four people. This would have been an extravagant option even for the Carnarvons, who most likely traveled upriver by rail.

Railroads had first appeared in Egypt in 1851, when British engineer Robert Stephenson constructed a line from Rosetta in the Nile Delta to Alexandria, the first railroad in the Ottoman Empire. The Egyptian rail network spread by fits and starts, linking Cairo and Luxor in 1898. The service was comfortable and would have transported tourists—and the Carnarvons—to Upper Egypt within a couple of days. Traveling by rail had the advantage that one could book private first-class compartments and also carry large amounts of baggage. The Carnarvons with their elaborate wardrobes always traveled with numerous trunks.

They traveled from the Savoy Hotel in Cairo to another upscale establishment, the new Winter Palace Hotel on the bank of the Nile in Luxor. With its horseshoe terrace and magnificent gardens, this luxury caravanserai was the first high-end hotel in a town that was still small and ramshackle, designed for tourists who wanted to stay a while without the regimentation of a Cook's steamer, however civilized. A wealthy clientele stayed there, including "splendid specimens of young Englishmen" and "delicious . . . English girls."[5] The Winter Palace was soon the focus of the Luxor season and became the hotel of choice for many Egyptologists working on the west bank. It became a second home for Porchy and Almina, whose wardrobes were the talk of Luxor. The pellucid sunsets that cast the western hills in luminous red-pink were famous and still are, but Luxor is now a bustling city with traffic jams.

Digging Begins

Carnarvon was impatient to start work, bursting with enthusiasm and delighted to have found a way out of his boring social routine. He must have wasted no time in getting in touch with Weigall, perhaps over a drink on the Winter Palace terrace, where last-minute logistical details would have been ironed out. Easygoing with other gentlemen, and Weigall was certainly that, Porchy must have displayed his more aggressive side, his intention of starting work at once. By the time he arrived, the inspector would have arranged for trusted *reises* and a sizable labor force, many of them from Qurna and veterans of other excavations.

Porchy seems to have been unfazed by the prospect of managing a crowd of laborers through intermediaries. Highclere Castle had dozens of servants, gardeners, and farm laborers to whom the Earl was a distant, but benevolent, figure. He is said to have gotten on well with his staff, many of whom worked for the estate for decades. The necropolis was a different matter. Here the intermediaries had but rudimentary English. The Earl had no Arabic and no intention of learning it. Nor did he have any understanding of the local villagers, whose world was as remote to him as life on another planet. He had to run his excavation with a gambler's passion, with decisive behavior and strong discipline, while remaining a remote authority figure. Like other foreigners, he would stand or sit watching the work, keeping an eye out for unexpected finds. The laborers were moving figures in huge, anonymous scenes played out on hot, dusty archaeological sites. They called Carnarvon "Lordy."

The two men crossed the Nile by private ferry, then mounted donkeys to carry them into the rubble strewn necropolis. They wound their way toward the low hills riddled with tombs and narrow defiles, passing Qurna's huddle of small mud brick houses. The necropolis was no longer the lawless wilderness it had been in Belzoni's time. Many important tombs now had iron doors. Inspectors checked on temples and sepulchers at regular intervals. As Carnarvon and Weigall wended their way across the rubble fields, Porchy scanned the landscape. "What's that?" he inquired, as they passed a small stone building. "A mortuary chapel, long emptied," Weigall replied. Carnarvon's enthusiasm must have imagined that undisturbed rich tombs lay on every side. He was wrong. Weigall must have warned him that season after season could pass without a single significant find.

"Here's your site," announced Weigall as they topped the low plateau. Carnarvon gazed out over a rubble field, not an imposing ruin or a tomb shaft, but yard after yard of yellow-brown, sandy rubble, littered with a few potsherds and not much else. It must have been at this moment that the reality of archaeology on the west bank sank in. This was no glamorous search for a royal tomb. Porchy confronted a desecrated burial ground that had been well picked over by generations of robbers and not a few archaeologists. He may have been discouraged, but his enthusiasm persisted. Within a few days the excavations began with a routine that continued for six long weeks.

Every morning at dawn, the *reises* and the laborers began work, the pace slow at first, then faster as the sun warmed. There was a rhythm to the digging. There had to be, for it was monotonous in the extreme. The excavation was never silent, alive with gossiping voices and laughter, even occasional singing. An experienced foreman knew well how to keep the men working. Everyone kept a sharp eye out for significant finds, for they knew that they would receive a small baksheesh (tip) for anything deemed of importance—to the point that there was an informal scale of payment for different artifacts. Clouds of yellow-brown dust rose above the excavation, blown before the winter wind. Fine sand made its way into every crevice.

Meanwhile, Carnarvon wakened in a different world of cosseted luxury. He would have breakfasted with Almina on the terrace outside their room overlooking the river. Dressed in a tailored suit with vest and tie, hat on his head, he would walk down to the landing place where the ferry would take him over to the landing place. A donkey ride, then his day began. A large tent with netting sides to keep off the flies stood at a strategic vantage point where the Earl could sit in comfort and survey the work. A servant hovered nearby ready to serve a cooling drink or a lunch prepared by the hotel. On occasion, Porchy would have walked down to the trenches and inspected the work, but he had little idea what to look for. There was no systematic plan. He moved his men from one location to another in the hopes of making a spectacular find, but to no avail. For six weeks, Carnarvon returned to the excavation, day after day, tolerating the heat and the dust, returning tired and dusty each evening to the Winter Palace. There Almina awaited him, dressed to the nines, ready for the tiresome social round. Carnarvon had to suffer the monotonous routine of balls, dinners, and gatherings that were part of Luxor's fashionable winter season. On occasion, Almina accompanied him to the dig, dressed for a garden party not an excavation. She wore high-heeled shoes and jewelry that flashed in the sunlight. But she was soon bored and hated the dust and discomfort of the excavation.

Most of the time, Carnarvon was alone. For long hours, he stared out over the busy excavation, lost in thought. Day after day, the rubble yielded nothing. He got nowhere, with no return for his money. Sometimes, Weigall came out to visit the dig.[6] The excitement of the cat had long receded. "Where will I find something more?" Carnarvon asked. "Be patient." counseled Weigall, who, it must be confessed, knew that there was nothing to be found at the permitted location. To the inspector's surprise and perhaps chagrin, Porchy redoubled his "strenuous and dusty endeavors" with renewed enthusiasm, undiminished by the lack of valuable artifacts. He did come across the painted but looted tomb of Tetiky, a mayor of Thebes dating to about 1525 B.C. but did not clear it completely. The open air did his health good. He was a long way from the social niceties of the Winter Palace and seems to have shrugged off his solitary ordeal. Weigall commiserated with him on his utter failure. "I am keener than ever," Porchy announced. He talked of returning next season with a bounding eagerness that must have disconcerted the young inspector. His visitor had changed

As Porchy suffered in silence, he had had time to think, to realize that there was far more to Egyptology than just buried treasure. Instead of throwing up his hands in despair, he found himself wanting to return, his vague intentions of archaeology as a form of recreation shifting gear into a desire for more prolonged explorations in the future. A new determination fired his mind with an ambition not only to unearth fine antiquities, like a gambler craving profit, but also to experience years of excavation that would rival those of Theodore Davis. And, at the back of his mind, he became obsessed with taking over the concession for the Valley of the Kings, so he could make the ultimate discovery, an undisturbed royal tomb.

The Carnarvon Tablet

As it happened, Weigall had left Luxor toward the end of the 1907–1908 excavations. He returned to his office to find that Porchy had departed, leaving his finds in a basket on the floor. Weigall sorted through them, to find two halves of an inscribed, plaster-coated wooden tablet stuffed into the mouth of the basket.[7] The damage was modern, caused by one of the workers. The tablet bore hieroglyphic texts on both sides. Carnarvon could not, of course, read hieroglyphs, nor were any experts nearby when he found the tablet amid fragments of mummies and potsherds on a ledge near the entrance of a plundered tomb. Curious about the inscription, Weigall showed the tablet to an eminent hieroglyph expert, Englishman Alan Gardiner, who happened to be in Luxor. He deciphered the inscriptions. One side recorded the well-known sayings of an elderly sage named Ptahhotep, of the twenty-fifth century B.C., learned, as we have seen, by Tutankhaten when a boy. The other told of the successful rebellion by the pharaoh Khamose of Upper Egypt against the Asian Hyksos kings of the Delta, who had invaded and ruled Lower Egypt around 1640 B.C. and ruled for two and one-half centuries. Khamose boasted: "I stopped the Asiatics . . . I freed Egypt . . . I drove out him [the Hyksos ruler Teta] out, I hacked down his wall, I slew his people."[8] Unbeknown to the Earl, this priceless historical document was worth the price of the entire six-week excavation.

The decipherment of the Khamose inscription on what is now known as the Carnarvon Tablet must have been a defining moment for Porchy, once he learned of his find. Once again he realized the depth of his ignorance. "I don't know enough," he said to himself, and made an important decision. "I need an archaeologist to help me," he told his friends. Once again, he turned to Gaston Maspero, who had taken a look at his excavation methods and disapproved but who liked Carnarvon and encouraged an unemployed archaeologist named Howard Carter to work with him. The partnership between Porchy and a prickly artist turned archaeologist with an obsession was to make history.

Restorer of Amun

Year 1, fourth month of Akhet, day 19, under the Majesty of:
Horus: Strong Bull, pleasing of births
    Two Ladies Effective of laws, who placates the Two Lands
Golden Horus: Young of appearance, who pleases the Gods
Son of Re: Tutankhamun . . .

A great stela once stood in front of the left-hand pylon at the Temple of Amun at Karnak. At the top of the stela, Tutankhamun, identified by his official praise names, makes offerings to Amun and his wife, the mother goddess Mut. Queen Ankhesenamun stands behind him. A thirty-line inscription below the pharaoh states that he "restored everything that was ruined, to be a monument for ever and ever." A revealing statement follows: "He has vanquished chaos from the whole land and has restored *Ma'at* to her place . . . the whole land being made as it was at the time of creation."[1]

Then the inscription warms to its task. "Now when His Majesty arose as king the temples and the estates of the gods and goddesses from Elephantine to the marshes of the Delta had fallen into ruin . . . . Their shrines had fallen down and turned into ruin . . . . The land was in confusion and the gods had turned their backs on this land . . . Hearts were faint in bodies because everything that had been was destroyed." Here was the new official view of Akhenaten's spiritual revolution. The gods had deserted Egypt.

According to the stela, the pharaoh stepped forward to rebuild temples and sanctuaries devastated by Akhenaten. He offered nourishing foods to the deities and embarked on an extensive building program. "The gods and goddesses of the land are rejoicing in their hearts . . . the provinces all rejoice and celebrate . . . because good has come back into existence." On numerous statues of the gods and inscriptions, Tutankhamun is given credit for the restoration of Amun and the traditional religion of the Two Lands.

Of course the young monarch was not personally responsible, nor did he instigate the reforms. His actions reflected the policies of those who advised and stood beside him, especially two familiar figures—Ay and Horemheb, both military men.

The Rise of Horemheb

Little is known of Horemheb's ancestry, but he seems to have been born in northern Middle Egypt. Apparently he was a noble and served in the army with some distinction, but he remained in the background until Tutankhamun's accession to the throne.[2] Soldiers had long been conspicuous at Akhetaten, protecting the royal family and serving at court. Both Ay and Horemheb had been soldiers, but the former seems to have become more involved in civil affairs while the latter continued what was clearly a distinguished military career on both the administrative and combat sides. During Tutankhamun's reign he became a general, Chief Commander of the Lord of the Two Lands. Whereas Ay, with his earlier posts as Overseer of Horses was apparently a chariotry officer, the general was an infantry man. As the reign unfolded, the talented Horemheb became increasingly involved in administrative and political affairs, especially diplomacy. He may have changed his name from Paatenemheb ("Aten Is in Festival") to Horemheb ("Horus Is in Festival"). Early in Tutankhamun's reign, he became the Royal Spokesman for Foreign Affairs. He led a diplomatic mission to visit the governors of Nubia and welcomed the Nubian Prince of Miam [Aniba] to the pharaoh's court, an event commemorated in a vizier's tomb.

Horemheb's titles proliferated. Like the older Ay, he soon became a Fan-Bearer on the Right Side of the King, a trusted adviser, King's Deputy in the Entire Land, and Noble of Upper and Lower Egypt. Within a few years, Horemheb acquired a status equivalent to that of the pharaoh's oldest son. In political terms, he was a regent, "the one chosen by the king before the Two Lands to carry out the government of both river banks."[3] He must have been soft-spoken and politically adept, a trustworthy adviser who was careful not to overstep the mark. He seems to have been able to say anything to Tutankhamun, to have been a pacifier and speaker of soothing words. Compared with Ay, his titles were all-embracing. The older man seems to have preferred fewer honorifics, preferring above all God's Father, which highlighted his family relationship to Tutankhamun. Everyone was aware that Ay was the senior of the two, partly because of his age but also as father (or foster father) of Nefertiti. But Tutankhamun seems to have trusted and admired Horemheb and looked up to him.

Of Horemheb's numerous titles, the most significant was *iry-pat* ("Hereditary Prince"), a label that had profound implications for inheritance of the throne. Under ancient precedent, Horemheb, as holder of this title would succeed Tutankhamun as pharaoh if the king died childless. Nobody in the kingdom outranked him, not even the older Ay. He was effectively, and apparently legally, the chosen heir until the pharaoh became a father. As we shall see, Tutankhamun's unexpected death changed the succession equation while Horemheb was on campaign in Asia.

Restoration and Retaliation

Horemheb was a tough, efficient administrator, who began the process of restoring Egypt's traditional secular and religious institutions. He was responsible for major building and restoration works at Thebes and elsewhere in the kingdom, begun in Tutankhamun's reign in the name of the king and continued long after his death.[4] Amun's temple at Karnak received major attention, with the demolition of structures built by Akhenaten before his move downstream to Akhetaten. The blocks from these buildings formed part of a new colonnaded court, south of the main axis of the temple. Tutankhamun also commissioned an avenue of sphinxes that led to the nearby temple of Mut. Many of the sphinxes were secondhand, originally sculpted to represent Akhenaten or Nefertiti. They were decapitated, given new ram's heads, and adorned with a small figure of the new pharaoh. Ay finished the avenue after Tutankhamun's death. The Amun temple at Luxor also received attention, where Tutankhamun commissioned a restoration of Amenhotep III's entrance colonnade. He also reestablished the *Opet* festival, an annual ceremony in which the statue of Amun processed from Karnak to Luxor and the pharaoh made offerings to the god. The pharaoh resumed an abandoned work of Amenophis III, an ambitious depiction of the *Opet*, the greatest religious event of the Theban year, for the Luxor temple walls, but it wasn't completed until Horemheb's reign, years later.

These alone were major works. Simultaneously, the systematic replacement or repair of the images of Amun defaced by Akhenaten got under way immediately after the accession. So many depictions of Amun Re adorned the length and breadth of Egypt that only a small number had been repaired by the end of the reign. The process continued for centuries. This was a far more significant matter than merely restoring images of the god, for the move involved reaffirming the legitimacy of the pharaoh. The rear face of the one of the temple pylons at Karnak displays two figures of Amenhotep III, Tutankhamun's grandfather. Two small depictions of Tutankhamun were added behind the figures. Both were subsequently erased, probably by Horemheb when he became pharaoh, but they appear as ghostly images.

The amount of construction and refurbishment undertaken by Tutankhamun was staggering. Clearly his advisers moved decisively to reestablish the traditional religious establishment and the wealth in a land that supported the deities and their priests. Art styles changed gradually away from the naturalistic Amarna style to the more formal mode associated with Amun, but with some similarities lingering, notably in human expressions, which tend to be more informal. Poses were more relaxed, more rounded and sensual. The rebuilding extended to Memphis, Tutankhamun's base of operations, which rapidly regained its former prestige. It was from here that the pharaoh issued his famous Restoration Decree subsequently displayed at Karnak, as the northern city became a more equal partner with Thebes in the south. As always, the depredations of the pharaoh's successors have decimated the young king's building works, which survive only as fragments of inscribed blocks and occasional votive stelae. A stela tells us that the pharaoh ordered Maya, his long-serving Overseer of the Treasury, to raise taxes to pay for the work and divine offerings for the gods. Maya apparently traveled downstream from Aswan collecting the taxes, ensuring that the correct rituals unfolded, and reassuring the people about the king's intentions. Then as now, symbolism played well as public theater. As for the pharaoh, he received a title: "he who spent his life fashioning images of the gods."

Most of important of all, Akhetaten was no longer the residence of the court—or the site of the royal necropolis. The royal interments in the nearby mountains were relocated to the west bank opposite Thebes soon after Tutankhamun changed his name. The mummies of Akhenaten and Smenkhkare, as well as Queen Tiye, ended up in tomb KV55 in the Valley of the Kings, which was excavated by Theodore Davis and Edward Ayrton in 1907. Subsequently the tomb was opened and Akhenaten's body completely destroyed or moved, while Smenkhkare's was stripped of its identity, probably not long after the closure of Tutankhamun's sepulcher, after which a sudden flash flood covered the entrance. Any actions taken with Akhenaten's mummy probably occurred either in Ay's reign or during the early years of Horemheb's.

The Living Representative of the God

Ay and Horemheb ruled the kingdom on Tutankhamun's behalf, certainly during his early years on the throne, and perhaps for most of his reign. A hierarchy of officials served under them, starting with viziers for Upper and Lower Egypt, as was common practice at the time. A prominent courtier, Maya, served as Overseer of the Treasury and of Works in the Place of Eternity. He was responsible for taxation and divine offerings, assuming, perhaps, a leading role in theological restoration. He donated two superb funerary figures to the pharaoh's tomb and was an adept survivor. He served on into the reign of Horemheb. There were other prominent bureaucrats as well, among them Pay, known from his tomb at Saqqara, as an Overseer of the Cattle of Amun. Tutankhamun sat at the pinnacle of a smoothly functioning government, theoretically the decision maker but in fact virtually powerless because of his age and inexperience. He was a figurehead because of his extreme youth—and yet he was not.

The Two Lands formed a linear kingdom, extending from the Mediterranean upstream to the First Cataract at Aswan. Beyond lay Nubia, much of it under Egyptian domination after many centuries of sporadic warfare and attempts at colonization. Even with Akhenaten's efforts, there was no single Egyptian capital, despite some imposing cities such as Memphis and Thebes. These were royal cities, associated with the king, where he maintained a palace and where there were major temples as well as separate government quarters. Unfortunately, many centuries of construction, reuse of stone, and the use of mud bricks as fertilizer caused much of these cities to vanish long before modern times. So the picture we have of them is lamentably incomplete. However, scattered documents and inscriptions tell us something both of the cities and of the royal visitors.

The linearity of the kingdom meant that the pharaoh was constantly on the move, surrounded by his retinue. His visits up- and downstream were formal progresses, conducted by boat and accompanied by strong military escorts. These were journeys in state, with high officials and courtiers in attendance.[5] Tutankhamun would have landed at, say, Thebes and settled himself in a kiosk or carrying chair to be carried to his palace or the temple honored with his presence. Twelve men carried the kiosk set on a wooden platform, where the pharaoh sat on his throne. Elaborate decoration adorned the kiosk. Men walked in front of and behind the carriers, waving ostrich feathers on poles to cool the monarch. Priests walked in front, twisting their torsos to release incense that both purified the air and created pleasing distraction from the stink of the narrow city streets.

Tutankhamun sat high above the crowd, his throne swaying slightly with the movement of the carriers. A line of soldiers held back the crowds as he progressed through the narrow streets. This was one of the few occasions when the impressionable teenager would have caught a glimpse of real Egypt, of men and women going about their business, of jostling markets—vegetable sellers, butchers, people selling cloth. He would also have seen barbers and manicurists at work, activities recorded in tomb scenes from centuries earlier, but life had changed little for commoners in intervening generations. The young pharaoh would have gazed out the teeming city, at two- and three-story mud brick dwellings thrown together haphazardly, according to need. The alleyways would have been thick with discarded garbage, rotting vegetables and bones. Mangy dogs would be rooting for food at every turn. Tutankhamun would have glanced at busy urban scenes, repeated at every city he visited. He would, however, have remained impassive, looking ahead, unmoving, a godlike mortal progressing far above the urban fray, distanced carefully from the workaday world.

When Tutankhamun visited a temple, he was clearly the supreme authority. He was, after all, the living representative of Amun on earth. He would pass through the wooden doors of the enclosure wall as the priests and pilgrims made obeisance, then process between an avenue of sphinxes toward the brightly painted great pylons and through the temple gateway. There he would dismount and enter the temple, almost alone. Tutankhamun walked across the temple courtyard, then through the massive columns of the Hypostyle Hall, the pillars symbolic replicas of the papyrus stems that that grew around the primordial mound at the time of creation. After his slow progress and offerings, the pharaoh reached the wooden doors of the sanctuary, where Amun's sacred barque resided. Here it was always dark. Here he carried out the rituals that ensured the continued favor of the god. Afterward Tutankhamun would ride once again on his palanquin, or even—and he would have liked this—in his processional chariot to a nearby palace, often situated some distance from the city. Even there, reminders of his unique relationship with the gods surrounded the king. Almost invariably, the front façade of the palace enclosure wall served as a perch for the divine Horus falcon, God of the Sky and symbol of kingship.

On his restoration stela, Tutankhamun is described as "knowledgeable like Re, [ingenious] like Ptah, perceptive like Thoth, a decreer of laws, who is efficient of commands and excellent of statements."[6] In reality, like every ruler, his life revolved around unchanging routines involving cult rituals and other activities. He was the chief priest of all the gods and knew all the secret temple rites. So the pharaoh participated in festivals and feasts in honor of different deities and visiting the gods in their "residences" throughout the land. Tutankhamun would have attended the most important festivals in person, notably the *Opet* festival at Thebes, for it was in the Luxor temple that the pharaoh's *ka*, the divine essence that made the king the living incarnation of Horus, was united with his living body. When Tutankhamun processed from Karnak to the Luxor temple, then entered the shrine alone to offer food to Amun, his *ka* joined that of the god. He was then ritually recrowned with the White and Red Crowns of the Two Lands; his legitimacy was reaffirmed.

The young pharaoh's word was law, for his acts were considered divinely inspired. Clearly, however, it was not until several years had passed that Tutankhamun began to exercise even a modicum of his awesome authority. At first, his role must have been predominantly a ritual one, whereby he appeared and carried out the ancient prayers, offerings, and pronouncements that were always the task of the pharaoh. Every king ruled by precedent but was careful to discuss his commands and wishes with his senior officials before they were announced publically as a formal act. Just how much of a role individual rulers played in law making is unknown, but much must have depended on the extent to which a king played an active role in day-to-day affairs. For Tutankhamun, who was still a child when he acceded to the throne and was surrounded by powerful, ambitious men, it must have been difficult to assert his authority, even as he approached adulthood.

Checking the Hittites

Egypt was a great power in the Eastern Mediterranean world in Tutankhamun's time. As we have seen, the pharaoh was a key player in a delicate balance of power that involved the Hittites, in what is now Turkey; the kingdom of Mitanni, which straddled the Euphrates across present-day Syria and Northern Iraq; and numerous client city-states of Egypt in the Levant.[7] As far as one can discern, there were few, if any, military campaigns in the Levant during Akhenaten's reign. But according to the diplomatic cuneiform tablets from Akhetaten and Boghazkoy, Hittite King Shuppiluluiumash I nursed ambitious plans for expansion. He advanced against Mitanni, was repulsed, then attacked again in what the King called his Great Syrian War. Other ambitious leaders were also on the move, a development that alarmed Egyptian allies on the

Mediterranean coast, especially King Ribaddi of Byblos. A close ally of the pharaohs for many centuries, his city was the source of the famed cedars of Lebanon, much prized by the timber-hungry Egyptians. Ribaddi called on the pharaoh to intervene, but to no avail. Eventually Byblos fell and became allied to Kadesh, a Hittite vassal. Apparently, significant numbers of refugees flooded into Egypt. By the end of Akhenaten's reign, the Hittites had not attacked actual Egyptian colonies, but their client states in re-moter areas of Northern Syria passed under Shuppiluluiumash's rule. What Egyptolo-gist Aidan Dodson calls a "cold war" pertained between Egypt and Hatti, which may have prompted the Hittite ruler to write a letter to Tutankhamun on his accession: "Why, my brother, have you held back the presents that your father made to me when he was alive? Now you, my brother, have ascended the throne of your father, and, just as your father and I were desirous of peace between us, so now too should you and I be friendly with one another."[8]

The currency of diplomacy was not only political marriages of princesses to Egyp-tian kings but well-timed gifts. Tutankhamun's tomb contains diplomatic offerings— sandals of Asian design, linen socks, a tunic from Mitanni embroidered with his name and titles. Perhaps most valuable of all was a pair of daggers, the one with a silver blade, the other of iron. Both these metals were highly exotic at the time. A diplo-matic gift from a Syrian ruler may have been a long, braided hip wrap that is 3.1 meters (10 feet) long, fastened with a belt.

Soon afterward, the Hittites attacked cities in what is now Syria's Beqaa Valley, causing the ruler of Amurra, a long-term Egyptian ally, to transfer his loyalties to the Hittites. Egypt appeared impotent until General Horemheb intervened—if we are to believe scenes on the walls of his sepulcher that depict fleeing and butchered soldiers, Canaanite and Syrian captives, and a Hittite delegation asking for peace terms. We've already mentioned Tutankhamun's apparent love for chariots, depicted on a painted box from his tomb. One side shows the pharaoh conquering Asian foes. This could be a reflection of an eastern campaign during his reign, but it's only fair to point out that the other side of the box shows him symbolically overwhelming Nubian foes. A battle scene on Tutankhamun's monument at Karnak, painstakingly reconstructed from widely dispersed blocks, shows the pharaoh triumphing during what appears to be a successful Syrian operation, so there may be some truth in the laudatory inscriptions.

Horemheb may have organized and carried out the campaign, but it would have had to be sanctioned by Amun. This is where Tutankhamun would have come in. Ay and the general would have urged war, but the pharaoh not only had to approve, he also had to receive divine support. Tutankhamun would have entered the divine pres-ence, perhaps at Karnak or Luxor, made offerings and consulted the oracle. Judging from scenes from a later reign on the walls of the temple at Medinet Habu near The-bes, the king would have emerged from the temple carrying a sickle sword, a *khepesh*, received from the god.[9] He would have mounted his ceremonial chariot and reviewed the troops, preceded by another chariot bearing the standard of Amun. When the army returned with their booty, the pharaoh would have reviewed them, also the prisoners and spoils of war and publically offered them to Amun.

The Pharaoh Rebels?

Tutankhamun would not have accompanied the army on its campaign. Some military equipment came from his tomb, including a folding campaign bed and folding stools, and a sleeveless bodice made up of thick leather scales, of a type worn by earlier pharaohs. By the time war broke out, he would have been well into his teenage years, perhaps quick tempered and rebelling against his regimented life. Ay and Horemheb would have flatly told him that he was staying in Egypt. They would have pointed out, quite rightly, that he had important religious responsibilities at home; there was a country to be run, decisions to be made every day. There was, of course, an unspoken point—Tutankhamun with his clubfoot and stick would have been unusually susceptible to an accident or to capture when helpless. We can imagine a sudden burst of pharaonic anger: "How dare you tell me that I cannot go? I'm the one responsible for decisions here. *I've* decided that I'll go to battle."

The outburst was quite unlike the normal mien of the pharaoh, who was judicious, humble, and reasoned during royal audiences. Ay and Horemheb looked at each other. They had their disagreements, for both were ambitious courtiers with an eye to the future. Both knew they were dangerously close to breaching centuries-old protocol. However, Tutankhamun's outburst was a token of his youth and inexperience and of his growing frustration with his physical limitations.

Horemheb nodded slightly at Ay and spoke calmly, with all the subordination and tact of a loyal senior official. At the same time, he allowed a quiet, but unmistakable authority to creep into his voice. "Life! Prosperity! Health!" he murmured in ancient formality. "Ay, Father of the Gods, and I are your servants, loyal to Amun and to you, his beloved. On your shoulders lies the present and future of the Two Lands. You are the living presence of the God. Since you became king, you've worked hard to restore the ancient ways of Amun. This work is incomplete and cannot be completed without your presence, your intercession with the god. We respectfully submit that this god-given task is more important than conquering savage Syrians."

Tutankhamun gestured angrily. "My place is in my chariot at the head of my soldiers," he retorted. "I have the equipment, I can fire a bow, drive a chariot. I'm the king, a warrior like strong-armed Horus, lord of action. I'll return with prisoners and booty captured with my own hands. It is my decision."

Horemheb had witnessed battle at first hand and knew well the brutal reality. He reached back into the past, to comfortable precedent, which all pharaohs respected. He spoke soothingly. "You are the most powerful king on earth, the successor of great rulers who governed the Two Lands with serenity and justice. Some of them, older than you, were indeed successful in battle. If Amun grants you long life, you'll be a great pharaoh remembered and honored by the gods. My advice is to be patient, to wait, for this is not an important war, and there'll be others. I look forward to being led into battle by you when the right opportunity arises."

The argument must have continued with some vehemence on sides, in what must have been a private audience where opinions could be expressed freely. In the end, Tutankhamun seems to have given in, for there is no evidence he went on the battlefield.

How do we know that such confrontations took place? We don't, for sure. We have only the most indirect hint that Tutankhamun occasionally rebelled against his advisers. A fascinating phrase in the Coronation Stela erected by Horemheb when he became pharaoh talks about how "unique" were his gifts, apparently how diplomatic he was. "When he was summoned before the sovereign, the palace having fallen into rage, he opened his mouth and answered the king and made him happy with the speech of his mouth."[10] We cannot be absolutely sure that this refers to Tutankhamun or to his successor, Ay, but it would be surprising if the growing teenager, now married and feeling shunted aside, hadn't rebelled occasionally. He'd assumed grotesquely heavy responsibilities long before reaching adulthood. And his two senior advisers were determined to make decisions for him, even when he grew older. This must have become increasingly difficult as the years of the reign passed.

A Pawn in a Larger Game

Tutankhamun's decade on the throne spanned a period of major transition from the Amarna years, which must have been extremely treacherous, even for the traditionalists who prevailed. They desecrated Akhenaten's image wherever they could, erased inscriptions, and desecrated or pulled down his temples. By all indications, Ay and Horemheb were ruthless in their pursuit of continuity and tradition, because they realized that these principles were the strength of Egypt in an increasingly interconnected and volatile Eastern Mediterranean world. Tutankhamun was a pawn in their larger game, the pawn behind which they could take refuge if need be. His perceived secular and religious authority, honed by hundreds of years of carefully nurtured precedent, was their most powerful weapon of all, and they used it brilliantly to achieve their long-term goals.

Most of the activity during Tutankhamun's reign revolved around the implementation of the measures laid out in the Restoration Stela. The process was far from complete by his death and continued during ensuing reigns. It was a complex restoration, complicated by factionalism, intense debate, and perhaps even by violence. But the course set by Tutankhamun and his regents prevailed and was to sustain Egypt for another thousand years. This was this little known king's greatest achievement, even if it was carried out by others. Just renaming himself had enormous political and religious impact.

The pharaoh may have been a pawn, but one important task had to be taken in hand at once—the preparation of a sepulcher.[11] A tomb was an important symbol of continuity, of eternity, of a ruler passing from the living world to that of the gods. Constructing a resting place was an important ritual act, redolent with symbolism, begun soon after accession, because no one knew how long the king would reign, especially if he was frail, as was Tutankhamun. Burial in the hills near Akhetaten was unthinkable heresy, so his first tomb near there was abandoned. He needed a new resting place in the Valley of the Kings. Exactly when a site was selected and work began is uncertain—one suspects partly because of the difficulty of selecting a suitable location. Tutankhamun's grandfather, Amenhotep III, was buried in the hitherto empty western arm of the Valley of the Kings, which was where Amenhotep IV (Akhenaten) had originally planned his tomb, but work stopped when he moved to his new city. The unfinished burial place may have been selected for Tutankhamun, but it was never used. A new site nearby was chosen and excavation began, but it was incomplete at the time of the pharaoh's sudden death. A memorial temple was also part of the burial project, and this, too, was probably unfinished when he died. No trace of what would have been an imposing structure has ever been found, but most experts believe that it was planned for a location near Medinet Habu.

The events of Tutankhamun's reign are a ghostly palimpsest of incomplete inscriptions, a few scattered artifacts like ring bezels and molds found bearing his name at Akhetaten, and a scatter of artifacts from the Malqata palace near Thebes, where the king apparently spent periods of time. If he was like other pharaohs, he was constantly on the move, and, given the uncertainty of his times, this may have been a priority. After all, the pharaoh as a mortal filled with divine energy imparted to him at his coronation was a powerful presence, the "breath of life." Courtiers commemorated their closeness to the king on the walls of their sepulchers, their time in the presence of a pharaoh so divine that they were not permitted to touch him. Tutankhamun ("Effective for Amun") was the most powerful weapon that his ambitious and ruthless courtiers had at their disposal. Ay and Horemheb made decisions in his name and issued proclamations approved by their teenage ruler. They both knew, and probably the young king did as well, that the stakes for the Two Lands were far higher than their own roles. At play here were continuity, legitimacy, and the restoration of *ma'at*, rightness, the philosophical basis of an ancient and long-lived civilization ruled by ritual and long-established precedent.

The Search Narrows

"A good sort, but perfectly irresponsible." Arthur Weigall's verdict on Carnarvon's 1907–1908 excavations must have reached Gaston Maspero's ears.[1] For all we know, the inspector may have insisted that the concession be withdrawn or, as a condition of its renewal, that competent archaeological supervision be obtained. There was no way that Maspero could cancel the Earl's permit. Carnarvon was too well connected at the highest levels. After an unsuccessful season, the Earl himself had been thinking of professional assistance, even of bringing someone out from England. Such guidance would give his work professional credibility. Maspero thought immediately of Howard Carter, whom he held in high regard, currently unemployed. Laconic but plain speaking, obstinate but highly competent, the near-penniless Carter was an ideal, and convenient, solution, with advantages to both sides.[2] To work with Carnarvon provided a regular salary and fresh archaeological opportunities, also a chance to mingle socially with the wealthy and well connected, many of them enthusiastic collectors. Carter may have been a serious archaeologist, but he was also a dealer on the side, as were other professionals of the day.

What Weigall thought of the arrangement is unknown, but he certainly disapproved of the way in which the Earl had acquired his concession. Carnarvon himself had been thinking of moving his operations to Aswan upstream, where others had obtained good results, but he remained at the necropolis when Carter came aboard. In truth, the old ways of excavation used by Theodore Davis and others, and initially by Carnarvon, were an anachronism in an era of increased professionalism. Davis was very much a social excavator, leaving much of the dirty work to others. In contrast, Carnarvon and Carter were deeply committed to their excavations and supervised them carefully with long-term plans in mind. They worked in a well-explored area of the necropolis. Ultimately the excavations were a laborious task of clearance, of removing limestone chippings, flood debris, and spoil heaps from earlier excavations to see what lay underneath. There was no dissection of serried layers, just sifting through piles of debris in search of unexplored tombs.

Lord and Pharaoh by Brian Fagan,
pp. 97–104. © 2015 Left Coast Press, Inc. All rights reserved.

A Partnership Is Born

Carnarvon must have learned early on that Carter was a disciplined excavator. One can imagine the Earl in his three-piece suit and wide-brimmed hat looking over his concession with a nicely dressed Carter, resplendent in suit and bow tie.

"I think we should dig there and there," the Earl remarked, pointing to places suggested by his *reis*.

Carter shook his head. It was not in his nature to be deferential to aristocratic gentlemen.

"No," he replied firmly. "We select one area, then clear it to bedrock systematically with a long-term plan in mind. There's only one way to discover tombs and that is by clearing off the rubble and examining the bedrock for signs of disturbance."

"I'll pitch my tent here," said Carnarvon a few minutes later.

"No," said Carter for the second time. "We watch the workmen closely, otherwise they'll steal anything they find the moment we turn our backs."

The Earl was in no doubt from the beginning that Carter was in charge. He was shrewd enough to leave the details to his colleague—he had, after all, years of experience at delegating responsibilities on his estates. Carnarvon watched Carter at work and took his lessons to heart, especially his insistence on meticulous control over the excavations. The Earl, who may have learned something of this from his earlier excavations, took Carter's example to heart. He was to write: "I made it a rule that when a tomb was found, as few workmen as possible should be employed, and, in order that the opportunity for stealing should be reduced, no clearing of a chamber or pit was carried out unless Mr. Carter or I were present." Thus, he added, "nothing should escape us."[3]

A new chapter in Carnarvon excavations opened with Carter's arrival. In 1907–1908, the Earl had found the looted tomb of Tetiky, a mayor of Thebes early in the XVIII Dynasty (ca. 1525 B.C.). The next year, Carter completed the clearance of the sepulcher, recovering large quantities of pottery and poorly preserved mummies. They concentrated much of their effort in an area of the Dra Abu el-Naga, known for its vaulted tombs. Nearly three hundred men and boys labored to clear numerous sepulchers, most of them dating to the Middle Kingdom and early XVIII Dynasty (ca. 1700–1500 B.C.). Tomb robbers and white ants had wreaked havoc on what had once been rich burials, except for three sepulchers, which yielded richly painted coffins, small statues, cosmetic equipment, and a nice toilet box. This was difficult excavation. Many of the wooden objects that survived in the dry conditions were friable and crumbled to dust at a touch. Tomb 25 was especially hazardous, with fragments of a wooden box that could be removed only with "trowel, bellows, and sometimes a spoon." Every gust of wind brought sand cascading into the trench. Tomb 37, a large rock-cut sepulcher with eighteen openings, had become a repository for later burials. They recovered sixty-four coffins, some furniture, a scribe's outfit, and a silver-bronze statuette of a boy named Amenemhab, standing only 13 centimeters (5 inches) high, mounted on a wooden base.

An Automobile Accident

At this promising moment, fate intervened and nearly killed the Earl. From the earliest days of motorcars, Lord Carnarvon had been an enthusiastic "automobilist." He was an early owner and was fined on several occasions for exceeding the speed limit on public roads and endangering pedestrians at speeds as high as 20 miles an hour.[4] In late August 1909, he was traveling toward Schwalbach near Frankfurt in Germany along an empty road at some speed when he encountered a sudden rise. The car sailed over the crest and encountered a hitherto invisible dip where two bullock carts obstructed the highway. Carnarvon did the only thing he could to avoid a collision. He swerved for the grass verge hoping to avoid them, but one of the wheels caught a pile of stones, two tires burst, and the car turned over. The Earl's chauffeur Edward Trotman was flung clear, but Carnarvon was trapped under the automobile. After frantic efforts to free him, he was rushed to hospital with a concussion of the brain. His recovery was slow, requiring much bed rest, and seems to have had a permanent effect on his health. Hereafter, Carnarvon's health was always marginal, but he insisted on returning to Egypt for the 1910 winter season and the excavations.

Five Years' Exploration and a Castle

The unlikely partnership thrived from the beginning and blossomed into genuine friendship. The benefits, especially for Carter, were enormous. Their standards were much higher than those he had learned under Flinders Petrie or when exploring tombs with Davis. He was a providential colleague, if given to fits of temper. He had a priceless ability at recording even minute details with drawings in his own hand or with photographs. With the end of the 1911 season, the two men decided to step back and write a report on their work. Carnarvon was pleased with the finds, which were a good return on his investment. It was time to report on their discoveries.

Five Years' Exploration at Thebes: A Record of Work Done 1907–1911 was the result, published under both their names but owing much to Carter's hand. Specialist authors contributed essays on different aspects of the finds. *Five Years'* was much more valuable than the lavish volumes that Theodore Davis devoted to his Valley tombs. The report was well received, a tangible result of an enduring, close partnership. Carnarvon was much more hands on than he had been when directing his earlier work from the Winter Palace Hotel in Luxor. He was by any standards at the pinnacle of society but had an informal side to him that was out of character for many Edwardian aristocrats. He participated in the day-to-day routines of the excavations in ways that were unthinkable to his rival, Theodore Davis, who lived in comfort on his *dahabiyyah*. Carter developed a profound respect for his sponsor, who not only paid the bills but also acted as a sounding board and a confidante. Carnarvon admired Carter's archaeological skills and, above all, his instinct for discovery. A mixture of Carnarvon's penchant for risky gambles and Carter's unrivaled knowledge of the Theban Necropolis and the Valley of the Kings was to pay rich dividends.

They also shared a common interest in fine antiquities. Carter had long dealt in artifacts, but always with a discerning eye for the finest quality. Carnarvon's father had been interested in Egypt. His own interest in Egyptology may have begun with his contacts with American Jeremiah Lynch, whom he was to help export mummies with a quiet word to Lord Cromer. His excavations assumed that he would have a share of the finds for his private collection—and Maspero was generous, often too generous, in his divisions. For his part, Carter had developed extraordinary contacts both with dealers and with potential buyers through his work as Chief Inspector, and from when he made part of his living as a dealer himself. He dealt with private individuals and with institutions. At the time, authorized dealers, and he was one, could export antiquities provided they obtained a license for the transaction from the Antiquities Department. All too often, however, finds quietly left the country without the authorities being aware of them. As far as one can tell, however, Carter acted within the parameters of the law.

Carnarvon had exquisite taste and collected mainly small objects such as jewelry or small statuettes. Some of his acquisitions went to Highclere, others to the British Museum or the Metropolitan Museum of Fine Art in New York. He also sold larger finds such as mummies to recoup some of the costs of his excavations—as did everyone else at the time. All these dealings, not only by Carter and Carnarvon, caused tensions among Egyptologists of the day. The wholesale excavation and exportation of valuable finds sickened many of them, when the priority should have been conservation and recording. Arthur Weigall was especially incensed; he was austere in his views about excavation and did not get on well with Carter, who, it must be admitted, was sometimes a difficult person to deal with. The pressure of the inspectorate told on him. Just before war broke out in 1914, Weigall had a nervous breakdown and left Egypt.

By 1910, Carter had been working for the Earl for two seasons, in what was clearly destined to become a long-term collaboration. His archaeological roots lay on the west bank, and it was there that he built an imposing house that he designed himself.[5] Castle Carter rose at a conspicuous site with a clear view of the entrance to the Valley of the Kings, complete with a central hall with a dome. Carnarvon seems to have encouraged him, if not financially, certainly with a gift of red bricks with blackened surfaces from a brickworks near his estate at Bretby in Derbyshire. This generous, understated gesture ensured that the house would last—it still exists, has been restored as a museum, and is well worth a visit. Castle Carter was a gesture of a long-term commitment on the part of both men both to their partnership and, undoubtedly, to a long-term goal—to take over the concession in the Valley of the Kings. "It looked like the abode of an artist and a scholar," wrote one visitor of the day. Carter was to live there for much of the year for the rest of his life.

Waiting on the Valley

The partnership now faced a dilemma. Their present concession was reaching a point of diminishing returns for Carnarvon's investment—the same kinds of finds, serious limitations caused by widespread looting and the ravages of white ants. This was un-exciting territory, even for the most tenacious of excavators, but they couldn't aban-don their concession if they had any hope of moving into the Valley of the Kings. Carnarvon looked around for a second concession as a way of diversifying his ex-cavations. Carter suggested Dahshur in Lower Egypt, with its IV Dynasty pyramids and extensive necropolis, but the area was reserved for "official" excavations. Neither Carter nor Carnarvon could change Maspero's mind, so they moved to the Delta, a much less promising option. There were numerous, and much neglected, town sites there, which were under threat from agriculture and industry, but the returns were likely to be minimal. They chose Xois (Khasut or Sakha) in the middle of the Delta.[6] The city's 24-meter (80-feet) high mound offered considerable promise, having been the home of minor royalty between 1750 and 1600 B.C. A multitude of snakes and logistical challenges caused them to abandon the site with minimal results after only two weeks. Carter moved on to Tell el-Bayamon, the ancient city of Smabehdat close to the Mediterranean, an area of undulating mounds, some Roman, others Ptolemaic and earlier. He camped among the rushes, amid a multitude of birds, and numer-ous mosquitoes, finding it cooler than Upper Egypt. Unfortunately, Carnarvon could join him only for a short time, for he was laid up in Luxor with a "sort of influenza bronchitis." Such ailments became increasingly frequent, even in Egypt's dry winters, a result of his automobile accident. The excavation yielded some low-grade jewelry in a clay jar and a statue that many years later yielded confirmation that the city was indeed Smabehdat.

The Delta excavations were very expensive and yielded disappointingly little. They had kept some excavations going at the necropolis but were really waiting on events as Davis's Valley excavations proved less productive, to the disappointment of the always-impatient robber baron. He believed the Valley was exhausted, a be-lief shared by Gaston Maspero, who was about to retire from Egypt. However, Carter thought otherwise. He believed that a combination of the right mind set, persistence, and a systematic plan of attack would yield exciting results. Carter seems to have shared his beliefs with Carnarvon very early on in their relationship, which were based in part on his experience in the Valley working with Davis in 1902–1904 as well as his long exposure to local conditions. Carnarvon always had an eye for a gamble. He had complete trust in Carter's instincts and was eager for a turn at the Valley. Davis was elderly and sick. He relinquished his concession, which was granted to Carnarvon in June 1914, although the documents were not officially signed until April 1915. Now the Earl could focus his sponsorship on the most desirable potential discovery of all—a royal tomb.[7]

In 1915, Carter worked for a month on the known tomb of Amenophis III, recovering some wooden faces from *shabti* figures and other artifacts. (*Shabti* figures were servants for the deceased in the afterworld.) But he did not clear the entire tomb, perhaps because he felt it was not worth it. By this time World War I was well under way. Carter got sucked into some informal intelligence work, the nature of which remains a mystery. He may have acted at times as a courier but apparently had ample time to stay in the Castle, to paint and sketch, and to do some minor research. Until now, his focus had been spectacular finds, but it's clear that he was beginning to think more systematically about the Valley, since the dealer scene was quiet and excavations were over for the duration. He began to think of compiling an exhaustive catalogue of finds in the Royal Theban Necropolis. There's a clue to Carnarvon and Carter's thinking here, for they were clearly planning very thorough work in the Valley when excavation resumed.

By this time, Lord Carnarvon and the epigrapher Alan Gardiner had become friends after a period of coolness caused by the gossipy and mischievous Arthur Weigall, who was a master at bad-mouthing fellow Egyptologists and their sponsors. Gardiner had examined Carnarvon's Theban excavations in 1913 and had visited Highclere to see the Earl's collections, although he was nervous of developing close ties to a social world very different from his.[5] This talented Egyptologist, an outstanding expert on hieroglyphic scripts, now wanted to work with Carter. With Carnarvon's agreement, in 1916 he published a long and definitive study of the Carnarvon Tablet. During the war years, Gardiner kept Carter busy with all kinds of small projects, including a "perfectly delicious plan and section" of Ramesses IV's sepulcher (KV 2). He then commissioned him to draw the *Opet* relief in the colonnade of the Luxor temple commissioned by Amenophis III and Tutankhamun and finished by Horemheb, mentioned in Chapter 7. Gardiner clearly planned a lavish publication, but Carter gradually withdrew and never completed the work. He had no desire to become Gardiner's man in Luxor. He was firmly Carnarvon's partner with a careful eye for the future.

From all indications, Carter found life in wartime Egypt dull, except for purchasing antiquities as the market picked up in 1917. He was in an excellent position to get bargains from dealers in a depressed environment and may also have been on a retainer from the Earl. He entered into agreements with the Cleveland Museum of Art and the Metropolitan Museum in New York to acquire fine items on commission. Both arrangements proved profitable as the war came to a close, with the prospect of regular excavations. A new Director General of Antiquities, Pierre Lacau, had replaced Maspero in 1914. Preliminary impressions were favorable, but it soon became clear that Lacau was strongly interested in scientific investigation and would not be as amenable as Gaston Maspero.

Carter was stuck in Egypt from 1914 to 1918, except for one brief visit to England. Carnarvon spent the war years in a state of frustration, mostly at Highclere. His health precluded military service. He resisted proposals by his friend Lord Kitchener, recently Consul-General in Egypt and a good friend, to turn Highclere into a military hospital.

Almina overruled him. She was ecstatic at an opportunity to do something worthwhile instead of merely being a social wife bored by the dull routines of the Season, whether in London or in Cairo and Luxor. Financed by Alfred de Rothschild, she spent the war years running first Highclere Castle and then a house in London as officers' nursing homes.[9] By all accounts, she did a superb job. Meanwhile the Earl was struggling. His health deteriorated without the warm Egyptian winters, his other passion than archaeology, racing, was much curtailed and then forbidden altogether, and Almina's nursing homes were enormously expensive. Carnarvon was lonely with his wife constantly away and his son serving abroad in the cavalry. He was, however, elected to the prestigious and exclusive Jockey Club, which gave him profound satisfaction. The Earl also acquired another passion—photography, which he had already practiced in Egypt. His repertoire now extended from shots of tourists and archaeological sites to young women, often in provocative poses. By war's end, Victor Duleep Singh had died, also Alfred Rothschild, who left Almina much of his wealth and a magnificent London residence with its art collection. In 1919, the London hospital was closed and the Earl was finally able to contemplate a return to Egypt and a resumption of work in the Valley of the Kings.

Work in the Valley Begins

The Earl's health was much more unpredictable after his accident and the war years. In early 1918, he had emergency surgery for a septic appendix and recovered only slowly. There were archaeological difficulties emerging, too, notably in the person of Pierre Lacau, who was much more restrictive about the export of spectacular finds. Since the Earl had gambled large sums of money in his search for rich tombs, he was hesitant to continue without some guarantee of a return for his expenditures. Carter had started work on a small scale in 1917, close to the tomb of Ramesses VI (KV 9). Like Theodore Davis, his long-term plan was to clear the ground down to bedrock, He believed that this expensive and slow-moving strategy was the key to more discoveries. After two months, he had no encouraging finds to show for his laborious search. He looked for another concession for Carnarvon and suggested El-Amarna, Akhenaten's capital. Lacau turned him down on the grounds it was reserved for "official" excavations or, if a permit was granted to outsiders, to a scientific institution and "not a private individual." The writing was on the wall.

In late 1918, Carter tested the rock-cut tombs of the governors of Cusae, at Mir in Upper Egypt, dating to between about 1700 and 1875 B.C.[10] The sepulchers were much disturbed, the season lasted five weeks, and little came to light. The dig marked the first appearance of the engineer Alexander Callendar, a retired railroad engineer and friend of Carter's, who was to become his major assistant. Like the partnership's earlier digs in the Delta, the returns were negligible, as were the results from the first season in the Valley. It says much for Carnarvon's determination and confidence in his partner that he continued his sponsorship. From the Earl's perspective there was, of course, the element of a gamble, but the main benefits were the warm climate, the improvement of his delicate health, and the chance to do something congenial rather than merely enduring the social round.

A week's Valley excavation in 1919 cleared an area in front of the tomb of Thutmosis I (KV 36), some distance from the 1917 dig. It was a time of political upheaval, which probably curtailed the season, since Carter was involved in urgent work as a political officer. He spent time during the summers at Highclere, cataloguing the Earl's collections. He seems to have been at ease in these rarified surroundings with its shooting parties and lavish dinners. He was now so close to Carnarvon that the Earl's surgeon carried out gall bladder surgery on him. He recuperated at the Carnarvon London residence.

The Valley excavations continued each season. In 1920, three months of laborious clearance work near the entrance to the valley and close to the tomb of Ramesses VI yielded nothing. Lord Carnarvon was actively involved in the excavations for much of the season, staying at Castle Carter while the rest of his party resided in the Winter Palace Hotel. Lady Carnarvon and their daughter, Lady Evelyn Herbert, were of the party. In February, the first real find, a cache of thirteen fine alabaster vases, came to light near the entrance to the tomb of King Merneptah (KV 8). Almina insisted on digging out the vases with her own hands, vessels that contained the oils and other materials for embalming the pharaoh.

In December 1920, work resumed, but they were unable to dig near the workmen's' houses by the tomb of Ramesses VI, lest they cut into the main tourist track into the royal necropolis. Most of the season was at the end of the Valley near the sepulcher of Tuthmosis III (KV 34). Once again, the results were largely negative. Carter had stated at the beginning that there were areas covered by the spoil of previous excavators that had not been examined properly. As we've seen, Davis had found artifacts bearing the pharaoh's name and was convinced he had located the ravaged tomb. In 1909, Davis had unearthed a series of vessels that contained embalming materials, which he gave to the Metropolitan Museum at the insistence of Herbert Winlock, the Egyptologist at the Met. By the early 1920s he'd realized they were fragments of the funerary meal of Tutankhamun and had passed this information on to Carter.[11] These and other clues had convinced Carter that Tutankhamun's tomb awaited discovery.

During the summer of 1922, Carnarvon invited Carter to Highclere to discuss the future. He was concerned about the high expense of his sponsorship, which continued to yield no results. Carter believed they should continue their barren search until there was no ground left untouched. Carnarvon talked of excavating elsewhere. Carter pointed to a small area by Ramesses VI's tomb. He proposed removing the stone hut foundations during the off-season and clearing the final small area down to bedrock. The cost would be modest. He even offered to pay the expenses himself. Carnarvon finally agreed. It proved to be a momentous decision.

Chapter 9

Death of a Pharaoh

During the later years of his reign, Tutankhamun seems to have enjoyed generally good health. He was of slight build, about 1.67 meters (5 feet 5 inches) tall, about average for an Egyptian man of his time. He had a relatively narrow waist but rounded hips, with a narrow face marked by a conspicuous overbite, inherited from others in his family tree. Today's medical technology reveals that he was well nourished and in reasonably good but frail health, except for his clubfoot and mild cleft palate, with him from birth. He had a shaved head, commonplace among Egyptian men of the day, partly to combat lice.

Then Tutankhamun died, apparently suddenly, in 1323 B.C., at about the age of eighteen. Shelves of academic studies have speculated about the cause of his death. For years, the experts pointed to a large hole in the back of his skull and concluded he had been murdered. We now know that the "wound" was inflicted after death as part of the mummification process. Another popular theory relies on a virtual autopsy of the pharaoh's body, which revealed serious injuries down one side of his body. The researchers took the results to car crash investigators, who simulated a chariot crash. They theorize that the king died while on his knees when a chariot smashed into him. Many scholars accept this scenario, the accident happening during a desert hunt or when chariot racing on a racecourse carved out by his grandfather by the Malkata palace near Thebes.[1]

Whatever the cause of his demise, Tutankhamun suffered from serious physical impairments. Another recent virtual autopsy, which involved more than 2,000 computer scans, showed that only one of the bone breaks occurred before he died. The only fracture that occurred shortly before his death and before mummification was to his knee and that was a serious trauma. But did this result from a chariot crash? The latest autopsy reveals a man with genetic impairments inherited from his parents who were brother and sister. These included his clubfoot, which could have prevented him riding in a chariot. Or did it? Judging from the number of walking sticks in his sepul-

Lord and Pharaoh by Brian Fagan,
pp. 105–115. © 2015 Left Coast Press, Inc. All rights reserved.

cher, the pharaoh undoubtedly used them on numerous occasions. It would have been possible to modify a chariot so he could ride in it with a stick. For a pharaoh not to ride a chariot was probably unthinkable. If he did ride one, his vulnerability to being thrown from it or stumbling when mounting or dismounting would have been higher than usual. I believe there is some merit in the chariot accident theory.

DNA research conducted in 2010 showed that the pharaoh had malaria as well as a bone disorder resulting from inbreeding. He suffered from vascular bone necrosis, which leads in the long term to diminished blood supply, which leads to the weakening or destruction of tissues. At death, the pharaoh had a bone infection in his left second and third toe bones, a condition known as Köhler disease, named after a German radiologist. It's a rare bone disorder found mainly in young boys that causes pain and swelling. Tutankhamun would have limped badly, putting his weight on the side of his foot. Today, the condition is curable with rest and painkillers, but it seems to have persisted in this case. It's interesting that illustrations of the pharaoh during his reign sometimes depict him seated while hunting and in other energetic activities, as if he had had this condition for some time.

When the genetic researchers examined Tutankhamun's left cheek and neck, they detected areas of patchy skin, as if he had an inflamed mosquito bite. DNA typing of plasmodial DNA not only in Tutankhamun but also in the cavalryman Yuya and his wife, Tuya, whose daughter joined the royal line, shows that all of them had contracted *Malaria tropica*, the most severe form of the disease, at some point. Apparently Tutankhamun suffered from this vicious strain of the disease several times. Older people develop a partial immunity against the pathogen during their lives, especially if they live near such malaria-prone places as riverside marshes. Unlike the older queens, young Tutankhamun suffered from multiple disorders. He may have fallen or had an accident and soon afterward suffered an attack of malaria brought on by a mosquito bite. We will probably never know for sure what caused Tutankhamun's death, but the latest scenario seems reasonably convincing. Whatever the cause, the result was fatal and the pharaoh died unexpectedly.

The Matter of a Tomb

Whether due to a chariot accident or malaria, the pharaoh's sudden death must have thrown the measured plans for his eventual burial into disarray. Neither his tomb nor his mortuary temple was anything near finished. Tutankhamun was buried in what appears to have been a slightly extended private sepulcher (a few much-favored individuals were buried in the Valley alongside the pharaohs). One reason for suspecting this is because Yuya and Tuya's tomb, KV 46, is very similar to that of Tutankhamun's before it was quickly modified.

The necropolis authorities enlarged the tomb enough to accommodate a sunken burial chamber sufficiently large to hold the nested shrines that were the customarily protection for a royal sarcophagus. The remodeling was probably done during the 70-day waiting period between death and burial, although the length of the interregnum varied greatly, often for political reasons. Unlike the tombs of such pharaohs as Seti I, only the small burial chamber was painted. The artists must have worked fast and compressed the usual themes drastically. Tutankhamun appears in the presence of deities at one end of the chamber. A highly attenuated depiction of the Book of Amduat showed only the first hour. At the foot of the sarcophagus, the artists showed the mummy being dragged to the sepulcher, a scene unique in a royal tomb but often found in private ones.[2]

For all the haste of his interment, the king went to eternity accompanied by lavish offerings and furniture. Many of the items—for example, the funerary beds—were gilded, not just black varnished, as was normal. The priests recycled items intended earlier for other royal tombs, reworking them when it became apparent that they were not needed for their original owners. These included the middle of Tutankhamun's three coffins, originally fabricated for Smenkhkare, also a statuette of a king originally standing on a leopard that has notably female features, including breasts, and that may have been an image of the enigmatic Neferneferuaten, the putative Nefertiti as coregent. Tutankhamun's tomb contains an amazing mélange of objects magnificent and commonplace, ritual and personal, some cherished heirlooms. They included a lock of his grandmother Tiye's hair in a small coffin, an ointment vase bearing Amenhotep III's name, musical instruments, and two of Nefertiti's bangles. One forgets that Tutankhamun had lost virtually all his family except for a great uncle by age nine. We learn of his diet from offerings in the tomb. Boxes, many of them mislabeled, contained beef and geese, emmer wheat bread in the form of half a dozen oval loaves, a jar of honey, and the ingredients and grinding stones for making barley beer, a staple of Egyptian diet. Twenty-six amphorae contained the pharaoh's much ballyhooed wine cellar from at least four vineyards in the Delta.[3] Many centuries later, the Greek writer Athenaeus described Egyptian wines as "pale, aromatic, and mildly astringent." Two of the amphorae contained a mysterious alcoholic drink called *shedeh*, apparently a red wine that was heated and a great luxury.

Tutankhamun's Funeral

For all the confusion resulting from sudden death, the ancient royal funerary rituals kicked in immediately. We know of them from tomb paintings from earlier reigns. An elaborate procession drew the pharaoh on a bier from the place of his death to the bank of the Nile. Mourners wailed and lamented as the dead king processed to the river, accompanied by the chief embalmer, a priest who read the sacred texts and another one, the *sem* priest, who performed the burial rituals. A boat carried Tutankhamun majestically across the Nile to the west bank, a symbolic crossing into the realm of the dead. The king's body arrived at a temporary *seh-netjer* ("divine booth") near his now lost mortuary temple, where priests washed the corpse in natron, a natural dehydrating agent.[4]

Next came mummification in another structure, the *Per Nefer* ("House of Beauty"). The embalmers shaved the body and removed the king's brain with an iron hook through his nose. They poured copious resin into the skull through the nose cavity. An incision on the left side of the body allowed an embalmer to remove the viscera, which were embalmed separately, then carefully placed in four stone canopic jars, a different one being used for each organ. Only the heart remained in the body, for this was thought to be the "seat of the mind," required for the judgment of Tutankhamun before the god Osiris against a *ma'at* feather, the symbol of truth and rightness. Then the priests stuffed the body with packets of natron and placed others around it before leaving it to lose moisture for 30 to 40 days.

The priests then oiled the desiccated body, filling it out with cloth and other packing materials before bandaging it with multiple applications of aromatic unguents like spikenard, a process that took as long as 35 days. They folded Tutankhamun's arms over his chest, just as Osiris carried his flail and crook. Each limb was wrapped separately, his penis wrapped in an erect position. Golden stalls covered fingers and toes. A pair of golden sandals adorned his feet. As the entire body disappeared under bandages, the priests recited spells as they placed numerous amulets, jewelry, and a ceremonial golden dagger among them. Finally, they fitted the king's golden mask on his head over a linen sheet, to which they stitched golden hands holding the crook and flail and a human-headed gold pectoral of a *ba* bird, a symbol of personality. Four golden bands bearing passages from *The Book of the Dead* wrapped everything into place.

Then the pharaoh journeyed to his sepulcher on a sledge, High officials and professional mourners accompanied the procession. A line of bearers transported the precious funerary objects to be buried with the pharaoh. There were funerary ceremonies along the way, offerings were made, and there may even have been a communal meal before the offering vessels were smashed. We know from a painting in Tutankhamun's burial chamber that twelve men led his funeral cortege, including the king's two viziers and other high officials, with Horemheb at the rear. An inscription reads: "Nebkheperure. Come in peace! Oh God protector of the land."

We do not know how long the royal funeral lasted, but it may have been four days and four nights. The floral bouquets from the tomb, which, presumably, were fresh at the time of his burial date to March/April, suggesting a spring ceremony. Three ritual beds were found in the tomb, one adorned with hippo heads, another with those of a lion, a third with cows. Perhaps the hippo ate the king symbolically on the first night, the lion rejuvenated him on the second, and the cow gave birth to him in the Otherworld. We will never know. At the entrance of the tomb, further rituals ensued. The mummy was stood upright facing the sun. Now the *sem* priest used a special adze to touch the mummy's facemask, the ritual of Opening the Mouth, enabling the dead king to breathe and function in the afterlife.[5] The pharaoh's successor performed this

Figure 9.1   Ay performs the Opening of the Mouth ceremony on Tutankhamun's mummy, a scene de-picted on the wall of the pharaoh's burial chamber. This act established Ay's legitimacy as Tutankhamun's successor. © *Griffith Institute, University of Oxford*.

all-important ritual at royal funerals. In Tutankhamun's case, this was his aged coun-selor Ay, clad in a ruler's traditional leopard skin, depicted performing the ritual on the upright mummy on the wall of the king's burial chamber—and thereby legitimizing his succession.

Inside the tomb, four nested shrines lay ready for the burial chamber, constructed in sections and probably assembled after the sarcophagus was in position. The im-mense yellow quartzite sarcophagus and its red granite lid would have already been in the burial chamber as the funeral began. Four goddesses carved at the corners protect-ed the king. In Tutankhamun's case, the three coffins were carried into the small burial chamber, perhaps having been stored in a tent or the antechamber. In another sign of hasty preparations for the burial, the priests had to adze the feet of the third coffin, which did not fit into the sarcophagus. Copious unguents hid the scar. The priests now placed objects in their correct ritual positions and lowered the mummy and the three anthropoid coffins, the innermost of solid gold, into the sarcophagus. They assembled the shrines, sealed their doors and unfolded a suspended linen pall between the first and second ones. A small side chamber held a golden canopic chest, funerary boats, and other ritual artifacts, guarded by the jackal god Anubis seated on a gilded shrine with carrying poles. Once everything was in place, the priests erected and plastered a wall that made the chamber invisible, guarded by two black vanished and gilded guardian sentinels. Then they filled the antechamber with ritual offerings and with the pharaoh's possessions, everything from clothing and weapons to stools, thrones, and his chariots. After days of feverish work, the mortuary workers retreated and sealed the doorways with the pharaoh's seal and those of the Royal Necropolis. Tutankhamun's journey to eternity was begun, and life for the living continued. Robbers soon entered the tomb, so the priests filled the access passage with rubble, inadvertently burying the remnants of the funerary feast and debris from the tomb.

Ankhesenamun Seeks a New Husband

We will never know the nature of the relationship between Tutankhamun and his queen, Ankhesenamun. That it was an arranged marriage is certain, for the perpetuation of the royal line transcended any thoughts of spontaneous romance. We know that she was older than the pharaoh, that he cannot have consummated the marriage until he reached puberty, All we have are idyllic portraits, like the famous depiction of the royal couple on the back of a throne in the tomb. Whatever the circumstances, the marriage was clearly designed to produce a royal heir, in which the couple was unsuccessful—two stillborn children in his sepulcher testify to that. We can also be sure that she had no illusions as to what might happen if he died before her. If she was still of childbearing age, she would be married off, probably to his successor.

And die he did, leaving her perhaps desolated, but certainly with an uncertain future. She sat, a widow, in the midst of a court riven by plotting factions, at a time of political uncertainty. Tutankhamun died at a complex moment for Syria. Carchemish on the Euphrates River was the center of gravity of the Mitannian state, which was reasserting its authority after earlier reverses. The Hittites were preparing to besiege Carchemish in the late summer or fall before the pharaoh's burial when King Shuppiluliumash I received a letter from Ankhesenamun, which amazed him. This may date the king's death to about six months before his burial, which would leave a gap of about half a year between his death and interment. Such a long gap was not unusual and may have reflected the confusion caused by the pharaoh's unexpected death. But, as we shall see, there may have been other factors at play. (For the controversies surrounding this incident, see note 6).

A messenger from Queen Ankhesenamun suddenly arrived at the Hittite court. She wrote: "My husband died and I have no son. But they say, you have many sons. If you would send me one of your sons, he should become my husband. I do not want to take a servant of mine and make him my husband! I am afraid!"[6] Shuppiluliumash was surprised and taken aback by what was, by any standards, a remarkable departure from normal diplomatic protocol. He consulted his advisers and sent his chamberlain, Hattushaziti, to find out what was really happening. "Perhaps they are deceiving me; perhaps there is a son of their lord."

Hattushaziti returned the following spring, accompanied by Hani, an Egyptian courtier, who brought another letter from the queen, denying forcibly that she was trying to deceive him. "I have not written to any other land, I wrote to you! . . . Give me one of your sons; to me he will be husband, but in the name of Egypt he will be king!" Shuppiluliumash questioned Hani closely. He confirmed that the pharaoh had died childless. He stated that "we desire a son of our lord in the land of Egypt for kingship." The Hittite monarch would have been foolish to ignore such an opportunity. He was deeply suspicious of Egyptian motives and deliberated for months. Finally he decided to send one of his sons: "The land of Hatti [and] the land of Egypt will be in eternal friendship with each other."

What was really happening? Was summoning a Hittite prince to reign as pharaoh a decision by the Egyptian court as a whole? Or was it an initiative by a faction allied to the queen? Was Tutankhamun's funeral delayed to prevent an Egyptian candidate from presiding over the obsequies and becoming pharaoh and to allow for the arrival of a Hittite prince? We don't know. But we do know that the Hittite monarch sent one of his sons, Prince Zananzash, to Egypt. He died during the journey, either in the Syrian region or in Egypt itself. That he died is certain, but whether of plague or some other natural cause, or by assassination, is unknown. Most likely, he was assassinated, perhaps at the hands of those who opposed any thought of a foreigner assuming the throne of the Two Lands.

Shuppiluliumash mourned his son and believed that the Egyptians had committed the deed. Had the king moved faster, Zananzash might have arrived in Egypt and married the queen before any opposition crystallized. The long delay provided ample time for a powerful opposing faction at court to lay plans. Most likely, they pretended to know nothing of the queen's intentions. Instead, they quietly arranged for the Hittite candidate to be murdered, perhaps in an "accident." They gambled on the likelihood that Shuppiluliumash would be most unlikely to send another son, so an Egyptian candidate could come forward, bury Tutankhamun, and become pharaoh.

We don't know who was behind this shadowy crime, but the finger of suspicion points firmly at Horemheb. Both Ay and the general had been the powerful figures behind Tutankhamun's throne, the men with real power in the kingdom. Of the two, Ay had the best royal connections, so it would be logical for him, as the senior adviser, to take over the throne of a now extinct royal house. Ay, God's Father, was the older, more experienced man, perhaps closer to the deceased pharaoh than General Horemheb, who was often absent on diplomatic or military missions. A document in the Hittite archives has Ay as pharaoh denying that the Egyptians were responsible for the prince's death and calling for continued friendly diplomatic relations. Shuppiluliumash flatly disbelieved him. He "let his anger run away with him, and he went to war"—against Egyptian controlled lands in northern Syria.[7] He captured prisoners, who introduced plague into his kingdom. There was "a dying" that killed both the king himself and his successor.

What happened to Ankhesenamun? Much depends on whether Ay was aware of the Hittite letters or even agreed with her plan for the succession. The chances are that he did not. The queen was right in thinking that her life was in danger. Only one tiny piece of evidence documents her fate, a glass finger ring that joins Ankhesenamun's cartouche with the prenomen of Ay. This seems to indicate a marriage between them, the new pharaoh taking an additional wife after the early death of his son Nakhtmin, a general in Tutankhamun's court, for the purposes of producing an heir. If he did marry her, then she married her grandfather. Certainly, no heir transpired. The young queen vanishes from history, and we have no idea what happened to her.

Ay Becomes Pharaoh

Horemheb may have been in Syria when Tutankhamun died. We cannot be certain, but there was certainly unrest on the eastern frontiers of the kingdom. If he was behind the assassination his motives would have been simple—to ensure continuity without interference from Hatti. Doubtless he had personal ambitions, too, for the succession was in doubt. His rival was Ay, a rivalry that may have intensified during Tutankhamun's reign, when the two of them effectively ran Egypt. Without question, Horemheb was a very ambitious man, one of those individuals to whom power was an elixir. Ay may have been ambitious, which could have caused tension between the pharaoh's key advisers. The general had one advantage, that of age. Ay was an old man, but his royal connections were such that he could claim the throne. And when, as seems likely from the slender evidence of the finger ring, he married Ankhesenamun, his succession was guaranteed.

We can only guess at the scenario. Tutankhamun contracts malaria, while recovering from a broken thigh bone. He dies suddenly while General Horemheb is on campaign. Consternation ripples through the court as feverish preparations for the pharaoh's burial kick into gear. Ankhesenamun may have grieved for her husband, but she would have no illusions about another arranged marriage, perhaps to someone much older whom she disliked. She writes to Hatti, a diplomat from Shuppiluliumash arrives at court, she writes again more urgently. Both Ay and Horemheb get wind of the letters. Horemheb quietly arranges an assassination, but he is far from the corridors of power. Ay, God's Father, is a master of court politics and intrigue. He quickly marries a distraught Ankhesenamun and is crowned pharaoh. As his culminating act legitimizing himself, he performs the ceremony of the Opening of the Mouth in Tutankhamun's burial chamber. He is painted on the wall wearing the Blue Crown of monarchy, an unusual departure from more anonymous scenes of the ceremony that were routine in other royal tombs. Ay had worked hard to strengthen his position. By now, Horemheb may have violently disliked the new pharaoh. Wise in the ways of the court with its seething factions and constant jostling for position, he kept quiet and bided his time, assuming that the elderly Ay would not reign for long. Much of his time would have gone into continuing the restoration of traditional religion and building support among senior officials, on the assumption that Ay would die without a male heir.

Ay reigned for a mere four years. Many of the previous reign's officials continued in office, among them the treasurer Maya, who was still serving after Ay's death. The pharaoh continued some of the building and restoration projects begun by his predecessor, while necropolis officials embarked on the construction of his tomb in the West Valley of the Kings. The sepulcher is somewhat smaller than usual, perhaps reflecting Ay's advanced age. Like Tutankhamun's resting place, only the burial chamber walls were painted, perhaps by the same artist. Once again, only the first hour of the *Book of Amduat* appears, together with a depiction of the pharaoh spearing a hippopotamus and hunting birds from a canoe, while his Great Wife, Tey, looks on, an unusual depiction for a royal tomb. Ay's sarcophagus, found by Giovanni Belzoni in fragments in 1816, was of the same basic design as Tutankhamun's, protected at the corners by goddesses, somewhat emulating Akhenaten's, which, however, had Nefertiti protecting the king at the corners.

The elderly king died in his fourth regnal year, one would assume from natural causes, but the circumstances are unknown.[8] His burial is another matter. Soon after his interment, someone mutilated the figures and names of the king and queen on the walls. Belzoni found Ay's sarcophagus lid on the floor, as if it had been lifted off or even never put in place at all. When discovered, the sepulcher was almost empty, with none of the familiar *shabtis* or canopic chests. The only sign of a funeral that survived is a gilt copper rosette that might have adorned a funerary pall, as well as some fragments of wooden figures and broken pottery. As for Ay's mummy, nothing survives. Most likely, those who smashed his sarcophagus, defaced his name, ravaged the tomb, and also destroyed the pharaoh's body, to eliminate any memory of Horemheb's rival. That Horemheb hated Ay seems certain, given that he destroyed all traces of him systematically. Only Ay's mortuary temple survived; its foundation deposits lie close to Medinet Habu, where Tutankhamun planned his memorial. Presumably on the grounds of economy, Horemheb promptly took Ay's incomplete structure and finished it.[9]

Soon after his reign, Ay had been erased from history as part of a systematic attempt by the general to remove all traces of the Amarna pharaohs from the offering lists to royal ancestors, which jump from Amenhotep III direct to Horemheb. And, with the disappearance of Ankhesenamun—perhaps she did not survive Ay—the last of the Amarna bloodline vanished from history.

The Pharaoh Horemheb

Horemheb had bided his time, waiting on the inevitable death of his elderly colleague. There are suggestions that he disposed of Ay, but there is no evidence to support this hypothesis. His coronation inscription, which was widely disseminated along the Nile, described the new pharaoh as born with divine protection, especially that of Horus.

113

He was, the inscription tells us, "chief spokesman and prince of this whole land" for a considerable time. Then the god "desired to establish his son on his throne of eternity." Horus led him into the presence of Amun at Karnak to crown him.

All of this fits what limited information we have. However, was Horemheb nominated by Ay? Or did the general seize power claiming divine approval to do so? Was there a power struggle between Horemheb and other contenders? We will never know, but the coronation inscription makes it clear that he was crowned during the annual *Opet* festival in Thebes, where his royal names were promulgated. They included a Horus name, Strong Bull Penetrating of Plans and a Golden Falcon title, Contented with *Ma'at*, who Nurtures the Two Lands. He was Horemheb Beloved of Amun. He then progressed in triumph down the Nile "with the statue of Re Horakhty and set this land in order, organizing it as it had been in the time of Re." His wife Mutnodjmet accompanied him. Her pedigree is uncertain, but she may have been Nefertiti's sister, which might have strengthened her husband's claim to the throne, even if she was once associated with Akhenaten, being royalty by birth.

"Set this land in order": This sounds very much like Tutankhamun's Restoration Stela, which was probably a matter of intentional policy, a signal that the reforms begun by the boy king would continue uninterrupted. Judging from an edict published by the new pharaoh, displayed on a stela at Karnak, he inherited a state in sad disarray. Corruption was widespread. Tax collectors appropriated slaves to work for them. Officials stole food in the royal name. Horemheb was said to be so disgusted that he wrote out his edict in his own hand. He ordered severe punishments for convicted officials, including death, whippings, and the cutting off of noses. He commemorated its issue by a public appearance, distributing food to an assembled crowd, calling out recipients by name. "Listen to these commands which my person has made for the first time governing the whole land; when my person remembered these cases of oppression that occurred before this land."

"I have improved this entire land . . . I have sailed it . . . I have traveled it entirely in its midst." How serious the corruption was and to what extent the state was in disarray is uncertain. We have only indirect hints, one of them being the hasty robbing of Tutankhamun's sepulcher, perhaps within days of his funeral. Then there were inevitable political fallouts from the Hittite assassination. Nor do we know if Horemheb was close to the throne during Ay's four years as pharaoh. Directly after his coronation, he seems to have embarked on a calculated mission to deface, erase, and destroy all traces of Ay on temples and inscriptions. He also usurped Tutankhamun's cartouches in prominent places such as Luxor, defacing statues and toppling them. Oddly enough, he left Tutankhamun's tomb intact, which is noteworthy, given that he strove to remove all traces of the Amarna rulers from official history. Perhaps he had a soft spot for the boy. At Akhetaten itself, he ordered the systematic demolition of Aten's temples, a process that continued after his death. Not everything was destruction. Horemheb commissioned three pylons at Karnak, using rubble from Akhetaten's destroyed temples as the cores. He also erected an enclosure wall for the resulting courtyard that showed captives from Syrian campaigns and a delegation from the Land of Punt at the south end of the Red Sea.

Horemheb had no living children, so he took care to groom a successor. He chose a vizier named Paramessu, who was the son of a troop commander. When promoted to high office, he became Noble in the Entire Land and Deputy of His Person in Upper and Lower Egypt, titles that Horemheb acquired during his time with Tutankhamun. The treasurer Maya continued to serve the pharaoh, as he had done since Tutankhamun's time. He was a favorite and presumably an old friend, who died in Year Nine of the reign.

How long Horemheb was on the throne is uncertain. It could have been as short as fourteen years but more likely between twenty-eight and thirty. Paramessu succeeded him, taking the name Rameses I. Like Horemheb, he was a former military man, so the tradition of military involvement in government continued into the XIX Dynasty. He was elderly and reigned for a mere two years, followed by two of Egypt's greatest pharaohs—Seti I and Ramesses II.

Unlike his predecessors, Horemheb was revered among earlier pharaohs. He appears in tomb chapels in the Theban Necropolis in the company of such luminaries as Amenhotep I. He was a deified king, his image carried during festivals such as that of one of the deities of creation, Min. He was part of the great succession of pharaohs of earlier history, a list that jumped from Amenhotep III to Horemheb. Of Akhenaten, Smenkhkare, Tutankhamun, and Ay, there was no mention in the King Lists. And yet, today, in one of history's striking ironies, the Amarna pharaohs are almost the most famous of all Egyptian kings. Tutankhamun's mask, the iconic sculpture of Nefertiti, scenes of Akhenaten and his family in the presence of Aten—these are as familiar to millions of people as the Mona Lisa. This resurrection of an obscure, almost unknown pharaoh came about because an Earl with a sense of entitlement and a penchant for risky gambles followed the instinct of an archaeologist and triumphed.

"I Have Got Tutankhamun!"

With another season guaranteed, Carter left England and arrived at Luxor on October 27, bringing with him an unusual pet—a canary in a gilded cage. Work started on November 1 in front of Ramesses VI's sepulcher. Three days later, the debris in the small triangular area had been cleared. Carter's long-term *reis*, Ahmed Gerigar, and his experienced workers began clearing the exposed flood deposits that covered the bedrock. When Carter arrived at the excavation, he was greeted by silence. The *reis* pointed to a rock-cut step, which both he and Carter knew was the entrance to a tomb. Carter went into high gear. The workers cleared the stairway, with Carter expecting a looted sepulcher. By afternoon, they had revealed a sealed doorway stamped with the necropolis seal. The jackal god Anubis, protector of the dead, sat above nine captives, representing Egypt's enemies. With admirable self-control, he filled the stairway with rubble, set guards on the tomb, and sent the most famous telegram in archaeological history to Carnarvon, who was still at Highclere: *"At last have made wonderful discovery in the Valley. A magnificent tomb with seals intact. Recovered same for your arrival. Congratulations. Carter."*[1]

Carter waited for three weeks, while Carnarvon and his daughter, Evelyn Herbert, traveled to Luxor. He spent the time making measured preparations for the clearance, and speculating as to whose mummy lay behind the door—if there was a coffin at all. Such careful, disciplined actions were the reason why Carter was so successful in the Tutankhamun affair, when others were anxious to tear into the tomb as fast as possible. He summoned Arthur Callendar from his home at Armant to assist him. Meanwhile, Carnarvon telephoned Alan Gardiner to ask if he thought his partner had found Tutankhamun. Gardiner replied that he would have to wait to find out. Both Carter and Carnarvon probably guessed that it was the obscure pharaoh's sepulcher. The Earl and Evelyn left for Cairo at once and arrived in the city on November 21, where Carter met them. On November 23, they arrived in Luxor. Meanwhile, Arthur Callendar had made preparations for the reclearance of the stairway. One of the most sensational days in twentieth century science was about to dawn.

Lord and Pharaoh by Brian Fagan,
pp. 117–126. © 2015 Left Coast Press, Inc. All rights reserved.

Figure 10.1 Lord Carnarvon, Lady Evelyn Herbert, and Howard Carter at the entrance to Tutankhamun's tomb, 1922. © *Heritage-Images.com*

November 24, 1922

Carnarvon and Lady Evelyn jounced on donkey back along the track that led from the Nile to the Valley of the Kings. They hunched against the morning chill, wrapped in thick coats against the north wind. Carnarvon and Carter rode side by side, a short distance ahead of the others, going somewhat faster than usual. They knew that a momentous day lay ahead. For the Earl, today was the culmination of a seven-year bet against scientific odds. For Howard Carter, the cool November day promised the archaeological discovery of a century.

The Doorway Revealed

"Callendar will have cleared the steps by now, so we should be able to remove the doorway without much delay. But first we'll have to clear down to floor level," Carter said.

The laconic Callendar, a highly competent retired railroad engineer, who had lived in Egypt for many years, was Carter's trusted assistant, who'd kept a close eye on the filled in stairway over the past three weeks.

"Why?" asked the impatient Carnarvon.

"We need to see if there are any royal seals on the plaster. That may tell us whose tomb it is. It was dark when I stopped digging."

The donkeys drew up beside a tent pitched near the tomb of Rameses VI. Carter helped Lady Evelyn dismount. Carnarvon had already shed his overcoat. Lighting a cigarette, he strode over to the workers clustered around the stairway heading into the solid rock. Basketboy after basketboy emerged with the last of the blocking rubble and tipped their loads well away from the stair. After a quick look, and a short conversation with Callendar, the three visitors retreated to the tent and drank tea. The morning wore on with an endless procession of baskets. Carnarvon fidgeted, lighting cigarette after cigarette. Lunch appeared. Everyone ate in silence. The Earl became ever more restless. His daughter told him to calm down, but he ignored her and paced up and down until he was covered with dust from the stairway. At last, in early afternoon, Callendar emerged.

"All clear," he said.

"Let's go down," said Carter.

The four of them descended with care. Carter offered a hand to Lady Evelyn, whose elegant but sensible black shoes were ill suited to the steps. The reis greeted them in the narrow defile blocked by the now exposed doorway. A small group of workmen crowded against the wall.

Carter took his flashlight and shined it across the plastered surface. The royal seals of the necropolis priests showed up on the stucco. He pointed out where his earlier work had ended, the place where he had probed under the wooden doorway lintel and seen a rubble-filled passage beyond. Now he could examine the entire doorway and pored over the surface. "Look, part of the doorway was opened and reopened twice," he said. "The necropolis guards must have resealed these small tunnels, for their seals lie above the repaired openings. There were ancient robbers here."

Carnarvon leaned down, following the roaming flashlight downward. "Look, more seals!"

Carter knelt and looked at them. "Tutankhamun!" he exclaimed. "This may be the tomb of Tutankhamun! If I'd seen these three weeks ago, I'd have slept much better."

Was this the sepulcher of one of Egypt's least-known pharaohs? If it was, it had been rifled, but not emptied, before Rameses VI was buried at a higher level nearby and all signs of the tomb obliterated in about 1133 B.C. Carter and Carnarvon looked at each other.

"Let's start now. Then we'll be sure," urged Carnarvon.

"No," said Carter. "It's late in the day and there's a mass of rubble in the passageway beyond."

Sensing Carnarvon's impatience, he turned to the doorway and levered out the dried clay he had used to seal his earlier probe. Hot air poured from the hole.

"Look at what lies beyond."

Carter shined his flashlight through the orifice and beckoned Carnarvon for a look. Then Lady Evelyn stood on tiptoe and peered through the hole. Dense rubble blocked a descending passageway 2 meters (7 feet) deep with the same dimensions as the entrance. The reluctant Earl agreed to wait until the next day. Apart from anything else, there was the matter of security. Callendar had already measured the doorway and had carpenters hard at work above ground building a stout wooden grille.

Baskets of finds recovered from the fill lay by the tent. Carter sorted through them with care, dividing a miscellany of objects into piles. He gave a running commentary as he worked. Alabaster jar fragments, pieces of painted clay vases, even leather bags used to bring water in to mix the plaster covering for the doorway. Broken wooden boxes bore the names of three pharaohs—Tutankhamun and his immediate predecessors, Akhenaten and Smenkhkare. There was even a scarab of an earlier king, Tuthmosis III, who had died a century earlier. As the afternoon shadows lengthened, the mood became pessimistic. The shattered debris hinted at a cache rather than an undisturbed burial.

Cache or undisturbed tomb? Were they about to find a mass of fine objects owned by earlier kings, brought by Tutankhamun from his predecessor's abandoned city, Ahketaten, downstream and buried for safety? Seven years of unsuccessful excavation were at stake. Carter and Carnarvon were well aware of the famous Deir el-Medina cache of forty years earlier, described in Chapter 2.

Memories of this spectacular discovery haunted Carnarvon's dreams. Perhaps Tutankhamun had brought a batch of fine objects owned by his predecessors from the abandoned city, Ahketaten, downstream and buried them for safety. Dare he hope that he would now come face to face with Tutankhamun? No one slept well that night, least of all the Earl.

November 25, 1922

The next morning, an impatient Carnarvon and Lady Evelyn watched as Carter photographed and recorded the seals on the doorway. He then gave orders to the waiting foreman. Workers with short crowbars chipped with care at the plaster coating, then levered the rough boulders of the doorway out of the way. Basketboys carried them up the sixteen steps into the brilliant sunlight.

The sweating Carnarvons retreated from the busy pit and sat in the nearby tent sipping coffee. Once more, a stream of laden baskets emerged from the stairway. Carter lingered underground as the doorway was removed, anxious to see if robbers had tunneled through the passageway. He identified two fillings. Dusty white chips filled much of the passage. As the workers cleared the rubble, Carter found traces of the funerary feast and debris from the tomb scattered on the floor. Clearly, the priests had filled the passageway after an initial robbery. Dark flint formed the higher part of the filling, where later robbers had dug an irregular tunnel that corresponded to a sealed hole in the doorway. But there were no signs that the tomb had been emptied. Perhaps the robbers had been caught red-handed.

At lunch, Carnarvon asked questions about the obscure, little-known pharaoh. There was little Carter could tell him. Tutankhamun had remained in the historical shadows for over three thousand years. All afternoon, both men flitted between the tent and the stairway. The nervous Earl fiddled with his hat and kicked at the dust. This was as stressful as waiting for one of his thoroughbreds to head down the final stretch, if not worse. He had run up significant debts and continued betting, often recklessly, even after he inherited the Earldom. He was lucky that his wife Almina's guardian had paid off his debts when they married in 1895. But he was still a gambler, attracted to the excitement of winning. And it was as a gambler, conscious or otherwise, that he had started digging along the Nile, betting that he would acquire spectacular treasures for his Highclere collection. Now, with Carter's encouragement, the stakes were even higher.

By sunset, Callendar had cleared much of the passageway. Progress had been slow as he and Carter sifted through the rubble to recover delicate finds such as broken alabaster vases. As they rode back to Carter's house when the men stopped work, the wooden barrier in place, and guards set, Carnarvon alternated between apprehension and excitement. He'd been a gambler all his life. Now his greatest and most expensive gamble of all was about to pay off. But he was apprehensive, too, prepared for failure. After all, his predecessor and nemesis, American millionaire Theodore Davis, had relinquished his permit to dig in the Valley and declared there was nothing more to be found.

"Wonderful Things"

Work resumed at sunrise under Callendar's watchful eye. The others turned up after a long breakfast. There was nothing to do until the diggers reached the end of the passage. The urge to plow ahead and see what lay beyond the rubble played on everyone's mind as meter after meter of the defile emerged from the rubble. Then, in early afternoon, 9 meters (30 feet) into the passageway, a second doorway appeared behind the diminishing rubble. With ill-concealed impatience, Carnarvon and Carter waited in the hot, crowded defile as a few workmen removed the last of the tailings. Basketboys brushed by them with heavy loads. Everyone was sweating in the dense, humid air below ground. Fine dust covered everything and caked on their faces. At last, the sealed doorway stood before them. Lady Evelyn slipped into the passage when the clearance ended. Carter examined the plaster with his torch, once again noting signs of earlier reopening. But the seals were intact, fainter than on the outer doorway, but they were those of Tutankhamun.

At this point, and after endless speculation, Carnarvon and Carter were convinced that a repository lay behind the doorway. With trembling hands, Carnarvon crowding behind him, Howard Carter made a small hole in the upper left-hand corner below the wooden lintel. He pushed an iron probe into the cavity. There was no rubble, just clear air. He lit a candle and held it close to the hole in case there were any dangerous gasses. Hot air escaped from the space behind. The light flickered. As the air stilled, Carter enlarged the hole and inserted the candle, Carnarvon, Lady Evelyn, and Callendar pressed close behind. At first the shimmering flame made it impossible to see anything. The flame settled. Carter's eyes became accustomed to the faint illumination. He found himself looking at a crowded room, everywhere the glint of fresh gold. Long seconds passed in astonished silence.

The silence was too much for the Earl. "Can you see anything?" he exclaimed.

"Yes, wonderful things," Carter gasped, struck almost dumb with amazement.[2] He widened the hole a little more so that they could both see in and inserted a flashlight. The bright light was the first to shine into the crowded chamber in more than 3,000 years. All four of them were overwhelmed with emotion and complex feelings. The sense of intrusion was almost overwhelming. Carter shined the beam of light on one group of objects, then another. Three great funerary beds adorned with animal heads cast grotesque shadows on the walls. Two life-size statues of a king in black with golden kilts faced each other, wearing gold sandals, carrying mace and staff, the sacred cobra on their foreheads. They seemed to be sentinels against a blank wall, seemingly a sealed barrier, surrounded by a host of smaller objects crowded into a small space— exquisite alabaster vases, painted and inlaid cabinets, carved chairs, even bouquets of flowers, a confusing array of dismantled chariots. An astounding treasure chamber lay beyond the doorway.

Some time passed before their excited minds could register that there was no coffin or mummy before them. Again the question: was this a cache or an undisturbed royal tomb? Then they noticed that there was another sealed doorway between the two black sentinels.

"That must lead to the burial chamber," Carter surmised. "There must be other rooms. In one of them, beyond any shadow of doubt, in all his magnificent panoply of death, the Pharaoh is lying." And, without question, that pharaoh was Tutankhamun.

It was too late for more exploration. The sense of intrusion, of stepping back into history, into the presence of a long-dead king, evoked powerful emotions in everyone's minds. They sealed up the doorway hole, locked the wooden grill, and once again left some of their trusted workers on guard for the night. Almost no one spoke as they rode their donkeys down the Valley.

Over dinner, they learned that each of them had seen different things. Conversation focused on the sealed doorway between the two sentinels. Was there a single chamber containing the sarcophagus and the pharaoh? Or was it part of something more complex? Carter, with his many years of experience in the Valley, argued for a succession of passages and chambers extending far underground, just like the sepul-

Figure 10.2 The antechamber of the tomb as originally discovered; funerary beds lie to the right, collapsed chariots to the left. © *Griffith Institute, University of Oxford.*

chers of Seti I and of other well-known pharaohs such as Rameses II. Perhaps he was wrong. Callendar pointed out that the design of Tutankhamun's tomb was completely different and on a much smaller scale. Whatever lay ahead, Carnarvon was elated and garrulous with excitement. Against long odds, he had achieved the archaeological equivalent of beating the bank at Monte Carlo. But he was worried, too. Had robbers beaten them to the punch? Visions of chambers crammed with treasure haunted his dreams as he, and everyone else, spent another uneasy night,

November 26, 1922

"The day of days," Howard Carter wrote of November 26 sometime later. And a day of days it was.[3] They were up early, for there was much to do. Callendar started laying wires to connect the tomb with the main lighting system already in the Valley. Meanwhile, Carter and Carnarvon recorded and photographed the seal impressions on the inner barrier. Both sweated in their suits and ties as the workers removed the boulders. They waited, almost in silence, until the task was completed, the floor examined for footprints. Then all four of them entered the antechamber of the tomb for a careful inspection. This time, they had powerful electric lights so they could see things that had escaped their notice the day before. They admired gold inlaid couches, thrones,

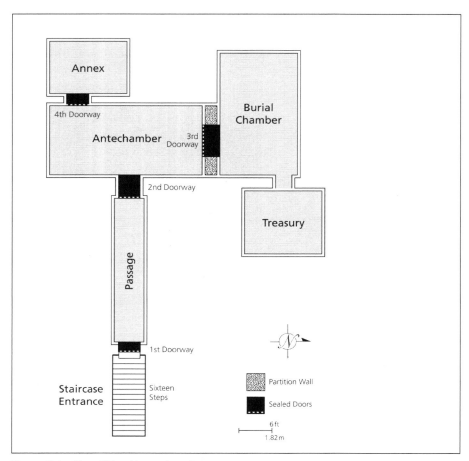

Figure 10.3 Plan of Tutankhamun's tomb.

boxes, stools, and sophisticated walking sticks. Tutankhamun's chariots leaned collapsed against the wall. Then came a disappointment. They discovered a small hole in the wall between the black sentinels, large enough to admit a boy or slender man, that had been resealed later. Once again, Carnarvon worried that others had been there before them and ravaged the burial.

For the moment, they put thoughts of the burial aside and made a minute examination of the antechamber. Carnarvon wanted to pick up artifacts, to admire their artistry, his collector's instincts aroused. Had he had his way, the tomb would have been cleared in a matter of days in an acquisitive frenzy, like that of his predecessors. Carter put his foot down.

"We must record everything, clear the tomb with the greatest care. Just the conservation of the smallest objects will be very difficult, for they are so fragile."

A reluctant Carnarvon nodded. This was going to be a long and challenging job—and then they faced the problem of removing the contents of the tomb and transporting everything to the Nile. In the end, the meticulous clearance took seven years.

They spent the rest of the day examining the packed chamber. Carnarvon's mind whirled as he pored over dozens of priceless and often unique objects that would have excited ecstasies of admiration as solitary finds. Here they were just a small part of a king's possessions.

"Just one of these things would be ample repayment for one season's work," he remarked. His gamble had paid off a hundredfold. The question was now by how much. He had never forgotten that his concession allowed him a share of the finds.

Some of the pharaoh's possessions were familiar from other sites, other finds. Others were unique, objects guessed at from fragments discovered in other tombs. The Earl was celebrated for his sophisticated artistic taste, but the antechamber amazed him with the vitality and animation of the art that adorned chests and even the smallest artifacts. Carter could read hieroglyphs, but Carnarvon could not. It was he who pointed out the frequent appearance of Tutankhamun's name on both large and smaller objects. By the end of the day, they were in no doubt that they had discovered the tomb of Tutankhamun, at the time an obscure and little-known pharaoh who reigned for a short time in the fourteenth century B.C.

For hours, exclamations of delight and surprise echoed through the antechamber, as everyone in turn drew attention to a new, spectacular artifact. Then a cry of surprise. When they peered under the southernmost of the three funerary beds, they noticed another sealed doorway. But the robber who had tunneled through it had never repaired the hole. Carter and Carnarvon lay down, worked their way under the couch and shined a portable light into another small chamber, again crammed with objects in complete disorder. While the necropolis priests had made some effort to tidy up the antechamber, it was as if an earthquake had shaken the contents of this smaller room. The robber or robbers had ransacked boxes, then passed some objects out to their colleagues in the antechamber, perhaps, also precious oils and unguents, leaving chaos and a debris-strewn floor behind them. There was no way an archaeologist could decipher the contents without weeks of work. So they admired some of the contents through the hole in the wall and left everything in place. Among them were a painted box, an ivory chair inlaid with gold and covered with leatherwork, and a series of magnificent alabaster and faience vases, also the king's personal *senet* board in carved and colored ivory.

November 27–28, 1922

As the extraordinary day came to a close, Carnarvon obsessed on what was the question of questions—what chambers lay beyond the two black sentinels? The conversation at dinner revolved around little else, what became known as the "Holy of Holies."

Someone must have asked: "What about making a small hole and seeing what's there?"

We don't know what transpired over dinner, but Carter must have urged caution. Carnarvon, impulsive gambler that he was, would have been all for a quick look. At some point, everyone agreed with him, if nothing else to settle the uncertainty as to what they had found. It was within their rights under Carnarvon's excavation permit to do so, but they agreed to keep quiet about it.[5] Both men were well aware of the furor that the announcement of the tomb would bring. If the burial chamber were opened with public knowledge, they would be overwhelmed with requests by people wanting to go in and would face even more complex security issues and hordes of journalists into the bargain. Their primary concern was to study and clear the sepulcher with the greatest care. In the end, the secret endured for almost a century, revealed by indirect hints culled from letters and diaries. We now know that Evelyn Herbert told Carnarvon's half-brother Alan about the foray as they were driving to the official opening of the burial chamber in February 1923, swearing him to complete secrecy. He recorded the conversation in his journal, which became public during the 1990s. A few workmen were also in the know, but they never said a word.

On November 28, the day before the official viewing of the antechamber by distinguished guests and high officials, the four rode back into the Valley after nightfall and slipped into the antechamber. Carter dismantled a portion of the wall between the two statues that had been resealed after an earlier, ancient entry. He confronted a huge gilded wooden shrine that almost filled the chamber but managed to squeeze into a narrow passageway between shrine and walls. Carnarvon and Lady Evelyn followed him, but Callendar was too large to do so. They noticed at once that ebony bolts secured the double doors at the east end of the shrine. Beyond it was another chamber, where the jackal god Anubis, guardian of the royal necropolis, watched over the pharaoh, wrapped in a linen cloth. Behind him was a bull's head on a stand, another symbol of the underworld. A single glance showed that the greatest treasures of all lay here, including ivory and wood caskets, also models of funerary boats. But, above all, the royal burial was undisturbed. After a few minutes, the three intruders wriggled out of the chamber. Carter resealed the small hole, hiding it behind a basket and discarded reeds.

A triumphant Carnarvon wrote in a letter to Alan Gardiner: "I have got Tutankhamun (that is certain) and I believe intact."[6]

Sheer persistence and a passion for high-risk gambles had put his name in the history books.

Aftermath

"I have got Tutankhamun!": life was never the same for Carnarvon or Carter after that magical day of discovery. For months, only the partners, Alexander Callendar, and Lady Evelyn knew that the undisturbed pharaoh lay beyond the antechamber. In retrospect, the surreptitious inspection at this critical juncture allowed quiet, measured planning of the clearance.

Two days after the first entry electric light illuminated the tomb, the cables connected by Callendar to the main Valley supply—installed by Carter two decades earlier. For the first time, they were able to inspect the jumbled treasures and offerings in the antechamber other than by flashlight. This was when the complexity of the task ahead fully sank in. The outer chamber was awash in gold and in utterly superb objects, including the famous chest showing Tutankhamun hunting and at war. The conservation issues alone were mind-boggling. Fortunately, Carnarvon's partner had long experience of presiding over spectacular discoveries and artifact conservation. He also had excellent contacts with fellow archaeologists working in Upper Egypt, with government chemists, and with the Metropolitan Museum of Fine Art.

Assembling a Team

As Carnarvon well knew, Howard Carter was obstinate and quick tempered when he did not get his way, which made him hard to deal with. Technically, he was the ideal person to clear Tutankhamun's tomb. As a public relations man and negotiator with bureaucrats, he was a disaster.

At first, things went well. The partners organized two official inspections of the antechamber, one mainly for senior Egyptian officials, the other for Pierre Lacau and his superior.[1] There was also the matter of publicity.[2] Carnarvon was accustomed to reading The Times, then the most influential newspaper in the world. Instead of arranging a press viewing, he invited Arthur Merton, a representative of The Times to be present. Merton's exclusive dispatch, published on November 30, was the first truly global announcement of the discovery. Lacau wrote Carnarvon a fulsome letter of congratulations on behalf of the government, but the Earl, rankled by the denial of his Amarna concession, didn't trust him.

The euphoria over the discovery now gave way to long discussions between the partners in the Winter Palace Hotel and at Castle Carter. Carnarvon had always been somewhat cavalier about money. He lived in grand style on a huge estate, cushioned from economic reality by real estate holdings, coal mines, and Almina's inheritance, despite evidence of financial stress caused by their extravagant ways and the expenses of the war years. Clearing the tomb would involve prolonged outlay, but the Earl assumed that the rewards down the line would be enormous, once he acquired his share of the contents, as allowed for in the Maspero concession.

"This is going to take years," remarked Carter as they drank coffee at the Castle in the morning sunlight.

"I agree, but it's going to be worth it," the Earl replied. The two men looked at each other and nodded. Both were collectors, with a close appreciation of the potential value of Carnarvon's share. At this stage, they both assumed the *partage*, a formal division of the finds, would go ahead.

"Callendar is a good man but no expert," Carter said. "I need extra staff, people who know what they are doing. Just stabilizing the furniture will take weeks and delicate hands. What about the clothes, the textiles, and the jewelry? These finds are unique and priceless."

Carnarvon nodded vaguely. This was unfamiliar territory for him.

Carter talked names, invoking connections he had developed over many years. "There's Alfred Lucas, the government chemist. He's an expert on ancient raw materials. If I can locate Harry Burton, the photographer chap who works for the Met, he would be perfect. Then there's Alfred Mace, who also works for the Met. He's a really good man with a lot of experience. And he doesn't get rattled."

"Let me talk to Lythgoe," said Carnarvon.[3] I'm sure he'll help us, especially if we assure him of some material reward." The proposed talk proved unnecessary.

The tomb entrance refilled and under heavy guard, the action now shifted to Cairo. Carter went shopping for people and supplies. Experts proved easy to attract. His reputation helped, as did the cachet of the Carnarvon name. He duly recruited Alfred Lucas, who served tirelessly as a technical expert throughout the clearance. He later wrote *Ancient Egyptian Materials and Industries*, a long, classic study based in considerable part on the tomb finds, which was last revised in 1962 and is still in print. By chance, Carter encountered Harry Burton and his flamboyant wife, Missie, in Cairo. All three had lunch with Carnarvon, and his involvement was apparently settled. Carter cabled Albert Lythgoe, who was in London. The Met man immediately telegraphed lending Burton and offering any other help needed. Lythgoe's telegram arrived before Carnarvon left Cairo. Evelyn described how the Earl was "deeply touched and relieved." The complexity of the task ahead was weighing on his mind.

Arthur Mace joined the team with Lythgoe's enthusiastic approval.[4] Lythgoe discussed the problems of the tomb thoroughly with Mace before he sailed for Egypt. He stressed Mace's patience and skill to the Earl. He was to prove one of the most important members of the extraordinary team Carnarvon and Carter assembled and was with the clearance to the end, helping Carter to write his popular account of the tomb. The Met also provided two architectural draftsman to draw detailed plans of the antechamber and its artifacts while they were in place. With Alan Gardiner at hand to advise on inscriptions, the assembled experts represented about the best possible talent to clear the tomb.

Not that Lythgoe didn't have ulterior motives. He assumed that the Met would receive some of the finds for its collections, having been assured privately by Carnarvon that he would receive some of his share of the artifacts, saying that the museum would be "well taken care of." The Met's help would give it an advantage over other institutions such as the British Museum, who would also benefit from the Earl's putative share. However, Lythgoe, for all his vested interest, emphasized to Carnarvon that the eyes of the world were on him, that the clearance must be measured, and that he had what he called a *"perfect* working machine" to do the job.

Carter moved fast. By December 17 he was back in the Valley with a stout iron gate to fit the entrance. He had also received permission to use two empty, little-visited tombs as a darkroom and workshop. The team set to work on the antechamber. It took two months to clear the cramped, hot, and jumbled repository. The process was far from harmonious. Carter had worked alone for years and found it hard to work closely with others. Tempers were frayed, but in the end, professionalism prevailed.

"The Times Is after All the Best Newspaper in the World"

In London, Carnarvon was the hero of the hour. King George V and Queen Mary accorded him the honor of a private audience. He discussed the discovery with Alan Gardiner, the epigrapher, also with Albert Lythgoe, who was still in London. He also talked at length to The Times.

The announcement of the discovery had unleashed a media frenzy that brought flocks of journalists to the Valley, crowding on the archaeologists, shouting questions. Carter arranged a press viewing of the antechamber on December 23, just before serious work began. This may have been the moment when Carnarvon, now far from Luxor, realized that Tutankhamun offered a remarkable opportunity to make money and to recoup some of his expenditure over past seasons. He was conflicted. On the one hand he wanted to do the "right thing"; on the other, he wanted to protect what he saw as an investment. He was pondering his options when the editor of The Times proposed an exclusive arrangement with his paper. Both Carnarvon and Gardiner went to see the Secretary of the Royal Geographical Society, who had benefitted from a similar arrangement over its 1921 Mt. Everest expedition, despite outraged complaints from other newspapers. There was also the possibility of a film contract. The Earl had dreams of ten to twenty thousand pounds, a fortune by the standards of the day. The Earl wrote a long letter to Carter, outlining the problem of press coverage, well aware that neither of them had any experience of dealing with the media. In the letter, he remarked that "I think the *Daily Mail* would give more, but *The Times* is after all the best newspaper in the world."[5]

Early in January 1924, Carnarvon signed an agreement with *The Times*. His ultimate concern beyond money was clearly one of control, a fear, also, that the discovery would become too commercial. It turned out to be a serious blunder. The press was up in arms, especially the native Egyptian media, which were very sensitive to an Egyptian find being handled by foreigners. Carter tried to calm things down by making *The Times* man, Arthur Merton, a member of his team, but this did not work. Then Arthur Weigall. the former antiquities inspector, arrived in the Valley as a special correspondent for the *Daily Mail*. He'd expected to be welcomed with open arms but was not, and soon he became a vocal critic and part of the constant guerilla warfare on the part of journalists besieging the tomb. Mace dismissed him as "fat and oily." He described how journalists lurked in the Winter Palace Hotel, constantly looking for someone to interview.

Carnarvon returned to Luxor in late January. By then, the situation was almost out of hand. His presence added a new social dimension to the media siege. The Earl was at the pinnacle of the social pyramid. Those with access to him begged for introductions to Carter so they could visit the tomb. Wealthy, patrician American supporters of the Met felt they had privileged access. Relations between Carter and Carnarvon deteriorated significantly, both over the exclusive with *The Times* and over the Earl's constant preoccupation with his potential share of the finds. Arthur Mace remarked in his diary that "the Carnarvons are rather a nuisance. He potters about all day and will talk and ask questions and waste one's time." In truth, Carnarvon was completely out of his archaeological depth now that serious clearance and conservation was under way. Except for his money and social connections, he was increasingly a liability. The pressure of work and the many decisions that had to be made as the antechamber was cleared already stressed Carter. The constant visitors got on his nerves, as did the hovering Earl. Mace remarked, again in his dairy. "This afternoon I had standing around watching me work an earl, a lady, a sir, and two honourables. A beastly nuisance they are, too."[6]

Tensions rose even higher when the antechamber was cleared and the finds taken to the empty tomb of Seti II (KV 15). There Lucas and others carried out at least preliminary conservation of the larger objects and packed the finds for transport to Cairo. Thick crowds and aggressive journalists crowded around the entrance as object after object left the tomb on wooden trays. Camera shutters clicked, and the press shouted

Figure 11.1 Two sentinels guard the walled-up entrance to the burial chamber; the outer shrine appears in the opening. © *Griffith Institute, University of Oxford.*

questions that were ignored. The suspense rose when it became clear that the day for opening the burial chamber was nigh. By this time Carter was close to a complete meltdown. There were harsh words between archaeologist and Earl. The partnership frayed considerably as Carnarvon realized that his excavation, sponsored as a gamble for fine antiquities, was turning into a scientific enterprise, with spectacular artifacts that ethically belonged to Egypt. He also realized that Carter now believed that everything from the tomb should stay in its native land.

Opening the Burial Chamber

On February 16 1924, the formal opening of the Burial Chamber took place in front of a small, distinguished audience. There were speeches; then Carter and Mace removed the first blocks of the wall, and the outermost shrine came into view. The press had been agog for days, lest there had been a secret opening. They were taken by surprise when the opening was a choreographed, formal afternoon event staged after a sit-down lunch and a procession of dignitaries to the tomb. It was too late for dispatches. In the antechamber, Callendar had boarded up the two black statues that guarded the burial chamber and built a low stage so that the blocks could be removed from the top. It took two hours to remove and pass them hand to hand out of the sepulcher.

131

Figure 11.2 Howard Carter looks through a shrine door. © *Griffith Institute, University of Oxford.*

When the hole was large enough, Carter entered, followed by Carnarvon and Lacau, Lady Evelyn and Sir William Garstin, who had arranged a permit for the Earl nearly twenty years before. Everyone squeezed through the narrow defile between the wall and the shrines, admired the second sealed shrine and the linen pall above it. They could see into the small side chamber, named the treasury, where Tutankhamun's golden canopic shrine with its four protective goddesses lay guarded by the jackal god Anubis on a sled. Jars, piled up funerary boats, a cow's head in honor of the cow goddess Hathor, an Osiris bed for eternity—the religious artifacts in the treasury were dazzling. Those who entered the uncleared burial chamber never forgot it. When people emerged from the chamber, "each had a dazed, bewildered look in his eyes, and each in turn, as he came out, threw up his hands before him." Carter called the wonders therein as "indescribable." "The emotions they raised in our minds were of too intimate a nature to communicate." Then he added what became famous words. "We had been present at the funeral of a king long dead and almost forgotten." Three hours after they filed into the tomb, the VIPs emerged into the open air, dirty, disheveled, looking at the Valley in a new way. As Carter said: "We had been given the Freedom."[7]

Figure 11.3 The jackal god Anubis draped in a cloth, guards the treasury. © *Griffith Institute, University of Oxford.*

Except for the signs of rapid entry soon after the funeral, perhaps by robbers in search of precious oils and jewelry, Tutankhamun's tomb was undisturbed. Carnarvon and Carter were both overwhelmed with emotion, the excitement almost too much for them.

A Fatal Bite

The pressure was unrelenting, with what one might call an official opening the following Sunday, attended by the British High Commissioner, Lord Allenby, and the Queen of the Belgians, who had traveled specially to Egypt to view the tomb. She ended up visiting the site four times and insisted on Mace opening one of the boxes for her. When the Queen left, Carter and Carnarvon closed the tomb for the season. Everyone needed a rest. Carter had the stress of the clearance and the constant bombardment of visitors. Carnarvon, who was not personally involved in the clearance of the antechamber, found himself importuned by people who knew him, or claimed to. As Egyptologist T. G. H. James argues, the tomb had become, in a sense, one of Carnarvon's estates. He was trapped by his social upbringing and position in society, which placed unsuspected demands on him. He seemed to have found some of the attention amusing, especially the journalists clustered in the Winter Palace. Those from *The Times* did their best to be helpful. The others, led by the disgruntled Weigall, spied from up close and from afar.[8]

Everyone fled. Carter isolated himself in his Castle. Carnarvon, Lady Evelyn, and Mace went off to Aswan for a break, sailing up the river, visiting tombs and the Aswan Dam. Mace described Carnarvon as "a queer old fish and in spite of his oddities very lovable."[9] Just before they left, Carter and Carnarvon had a violent quarrel in the Castle, which ended with Carter telling the Earl to leave his house and never return. There is no record of the argument, but it was almost certainly a collision of two contrasting personalities, which exploded from excessive stress. Carter was exhausted from running the clearance with all its problems and being engaged with pestering visitors at the same time. Carnarvon must have felt somewhat marginalized. He was not an archaeologist but, ultimately, a sponsor. Alan Gardiner and the American Egyptologist James Breasted succeeded in soothing the partners, but by no means completely. A week after the opening of the burial chamber, Carnarvon wrote a heartfelt letter to his partner. "I have been feeling very unhappy today, and I do not know what to think or do. . . . I have no doubt that I have done many foolish things and I am very sorry. . . . There is only one thing I want to say to you that I hope you will always remember—whatever your feelings are or will be for me in the future my affection for you will never change."[10] There is no record of Carter's reply—if any.

After a short break, the team resumed work in the tomb of Seti II, where they had some merciful relief from visitors and could get a great deal done. A century later, one is lost in admiration for the meticulous records that Carter and his colleagues maintained, preparing an archive that is still being mined by Egyptologists. Carnarvon hovered around the work, again getting in the way, for there was nothing for him to do. He had been bitten by a mosquito in his hotel at Aswan and had nicked the bite while shaving, but he seemed to be fine.

Carnarvon finally left the experts alone. He went to Cairo on March 14 to discuss future work on the tomb and the division of finds with Lacau but arrived feeling tired and depressed, complaining that his face was hurting. Four days later, Evelyn wrote to Carter reporting that her father was "very very seedy." He had a high temperature; his neck glands were swelling. A day later, she sent a cable to Lady Carnarvon as well as to Carter. Both left for Cairo at once. The bite had become infected. The blood poisoning had turned into pneumonia, a dangerous condition for someone like Carnarvon, who had fragile health at the best of times. Lady Evelyn sat by his bedside, but the Earl was philosophical. "I have heard the call. I am preparing," he said.[11] Lord Carnarvon died on April 5. Carter was in Cairo throughout the period of crisis, but no record survives of anything they said to each other as Carnarvon lay on his deathbed. Carter returned to Luxor looking stressed and exhausted. The family buried the Earl on the Highclere estate.

Thus ended a partnership that had lasted fourteen years, a relationship that began as one of employer and employee and matured into a genuine, close friendship. The two partners, from vastly different social backgrounds, had come to depend on each other in ways that they themselves may not have totally understood. Neither man had many friends; now the entire weight of the clearance lay on Carter's shoulders. He had relied on his aristocratic friend not only for an entrée into high society but also for a form of companionship and informality that lurked under Carnarvon's façade as a grandee of English society.

Controversy and Final Clearance

Howard Carter was alone, with Countess Almina and the Earl's executors in the background. He completed the actual clearance in 1929, at which point the countess decided not to renew the concession given to complete the work in 1923, probably on Carter's advice.[12] The six intervening years had proved difficult and traumatic for the excavators, with constant problems with the Egyptian government. Carter was never an easy man to deal with; nor was Pierre Lacau. At issue were several important problems that reflected the changing political realities in Egypt. One of them was the rights of the Carnarvon family to a share of the finds. Another was whether Carter, or maybe Egyptian excavators, would finish the clearance. Then there was the question of access to the tomb, which the Antiquities Department now removed from Carter's hands, even the keys to the door.

Carter finally snapped. Directly after he lifted the stone lid of the sarcophagus and revealed Tutankhamun's extraordinary gold portrait and coffin on February 24, 1924—in the presence of witnesses—he scheduled a press viewing and then announced that he was closing the tomb and stopping work "owing to impossible restrictions and discourtesies on the part of the Public Works Department and its Antiquities Service."[13] The team's wives could not even visit the sepulcher. Months passed in negotiations and threatened lawsuits, much of which revolved around the rights of the Carnarvons—the issue of *partage*, sharing the finds, in which, of course, the Met and other institutions had strong vested interests. A change of government in a more independent Cairo led to a series of meetings in early 1925. Agreement ensued. The British side renounced all rights to *partage*, while the Egyptian Government granted permission for the export of approved duplicate artifacts "without damage to science." On January 14, 1925, Almina Carnarvon signed a renunciation document. Nine days later, Carter was handed back the tomb "with great pomp."

Carter and his team now continued the methodical clearance, beginning with the burial chamber, then the treasury, and finally the annex. By now, the routine was well established—the recording and photographing of objects, their removal, then weeks of conservation work in Seti II's tomb, before workers trundled big crates on mining rail cars to the Nile. The big event was the pharaoh's mummy. Carter and Lucas untangled the bandages, a task that took four days. Powerful unguents had fried the linen wrappings, littered as they were with jewelry, ritual objects, even a dagger. In the

Figure 11.4   Howard Carter works on Tutankhamun's sarcophagus. © *Griffith Institute, University of Oxford.*

end, they had to remove the body in pieces, the head proving very difficult to separate from the golden mask. By today's standards, their methods were draconian. They even exposed the mummy to full sunlight for hours to help disengage the body, a technique that would horrify today's conservators. In the end, anatomist Douglas Derry decapitated the pharaoh, cut off his hands to remove his bracelets, and separated the hips, knees, and feet. The head was relatively well preserved, the face with "beautiful and well-formed features." Derry estimated that the pharaoh was about eighteen years old, but the state of the royal body was a great disappointment, caused by the corrosive effects of the unguents used by the embalmers.

And so the clearance of Tutankhamun's tomb came to an end, seven years after it began. In June 1930, the Egyptian government paid Lord Carnarvon's heirs the sum of £35,868 (about 2.3 million U.S. dollars today) to cover the expenses of clearing the tomb from its discovery until its completion in April 1929. Of this, Howard Carter received a quarter. The Metropolitan Museum received nothing for its expenditure.

Carter's thoughts now turned to a definitive, lavish publication about the tomb and the completion of the third volume of his popular account, *The Tomb of Tut.ankh. amen.* He was exhausted but toyed briefly with another project—and never began either work. In truth, Tutankhamun had reduced him to bad health and ultimately killed him. At his death in London on March 2, 1939, he was the most famous archaeologist in the world but not a loved one. Nor was he ever honored by the British government, which may have taken unspoken account of his lowly origins. Only Yale University honored him, with an honorary degree. A handful of people, including Lady Evelyn, attended the funeral of a man who once jokingly said that "I met just 78,642 people that winter [1923 or 1924] and showed the tomb to most of them."[14]

Egyptology since Tutankhamun

Howard Carter's work on Tutankhamun was a triumph, given the facilities available to him. Egyptology has come of age since the days of Flinders Petrie and casually trained archaeologists like Weigall and Carter. The expeditions of the Harvard archaeologist George Reisner, who worked on the Pyramids of Giza and in the Sudan, helped usher in the modern era.. He would have nothing to do with Carnarvon and Carter. The opportunistic University of Chicago Egyptologist Henry Breasted founded the university's Oriental Institute and the long-term project of recording inscriptions on standing monuments that began in 1929 and continues to this day. Egyptian scholars have become much more active. Egypt is no longer purely an archaeological playground for foreigners. Antiquities laws have been overhauled. Much emphasis now goes into survey and conservation. American Egyptologist Kent Weeks has founded the Theban Mapping Project to photograph and map every temple and tomb in the Theban Necropolis using hot air balloons and remote sensing to achieve what no earlier research could hope to do—a comprehensive understanding of the Valley of the Kings. The Project has also investigated KV 55, the vast tomb of Ramesses II's sons. Meanwhile, Greg and Sarah Parcak have used infrared satellite imagery to identify as many as seventeen pyramids and more than a thousand tombs—so far the results have not been checked on the ground.

As always, the Egyptologists labor in the shadows of political events—the Arab Spring, radical Islam, and widespread social unrest. They also work in an environment where surreptitious treasure hunting continues in an unending war between the government, dealers, and villagers with centuries of tomb robbing in their blood. Widespread rioting during the Arab Spring led to destruction in the Egyptian Museum in Cairo and to a surge in unchecked looting, which did incalculable damage. As stability has returned to the country and the government has regained control of antiquities, the brief orgy of illicit digging and burglary from museums has died down and once again gone underground. Nevertheless, as long as there is demand from collectors, the nighttime explorations will continue. In the end, the Egyptologists and government may prevail, but at enormous cost. Fortunately for archaeology, the triumph of Carnarvon and Carter's bold gamble placed the pharaohs on a world stage. Today, Tutankhamun is one of the major props of Egypt's economy, which depends heavily on international tourism. His sepulcher is in a fragile state and will be closed. Instead, near Castle Carter, visitors will be able to visit a stunning replica of the tomb in its heyday, which will give them a far more accurate impression of the sepulcher.

Two Men of Entitlement

This has been the story of two men born to extraordinary privilege and entitlement. Both lived their early lives isolated from the real world. Tutankhamun grew up in a court imbued with protocol and religious fanaticism, destined from birth to be a living god. Porchy came into the world at the summit of a carefully defined social pyramid, whose denizens moved freely and usually formally at the most rarified levels of English and European society. Pharaoh and Earl were never robust. The former suffered from the effects of inbreeding as a matter of pharaonic marital policies. Carnarvon had weak lungs and chronic respiratory ailments from birth that kept him frequently abed and sent him to Egypt's warm winters. In a fascinating historical coincidence, both died from the effects of mosquito bites, Tutankhamun from an infected limb fracture and malaria, the Earl from a bite that was cut while he was shaving and that turned into an infection leading to pneumonia.

Of the two, the pharaoh probably had a better education—if you judge education in terms of the very narrow definition of the Egyptian court. He was a rote learner, initiated at an early age in the innermost mysteries of Aten and the Egyptian cosmos. He was literate and knowledgeable about his role in government, even if his powerful officials and regents usurped his authority. The artifacts in his tomb reflect an interest in chariots, perhaps riding, and hunting. Almost certainly Carnarvon suffered from undiagnosed learning disabilities, which profoundly affected his performance in formal educational settings. Like most wealthy landowners of the day, he was passionate about horses and shooting and, like many of them, was an addicted gambler from his teenage years. Had the two ever met, they might well have shared their interests in horseflesh and hunting. In later life, the Earl educated himself in classic autodidactic fashion, through omnivorous reading. Perhaps the most important legacy of his education was an impeccable taste and an interest in art collecting, both of which came to a head in the Land of the Pharaohs.

Lord Carnarvon was a quiet, unobtrusive aristocrat, who was shy and not given to flamboyance. But he was a gambler, driven to make compulsive, risky bids. His decision to take up Egyptology was partly a way of escaping the tedious boredom of the fashionable winter social round during his enforced exile along the Nile. But distraction seems to have become a passion, fueled by one of the great partnerships of archaeology. Howard Carter had an obsessive belief in the existence of Tutankhamun's tomb. Carnarvon took the gamble and the gamble paid off—or did it?

It's impossible to compare Tutankhamun and Lord Carnarvon's characters, lives, and motivations in detail, separated as they are by more than 3,000 years. The young pharaoh was an obscure figure until the Earl came along, largely erased from history by the ambitious Horemheb. If his countenance is any judge, he may have been a quiet, sensitive person like the Earl. Like Carnarvon, he may have been given to fits of temper out of frustration and to feelings that he was left on the margins during his short reign. The Earl undoubtedly felt on the edge of things as Carter labored over the antechamber and burial chamber. In the end, their senses of entitlement may have meant relatively little in two very different worlds where momentous change was under way. They came together in death, the one discovering the other's sepulcher before succumbing himself to another Nile mosquito.

Carnarvon's bet never paid off in the way he had hoped and gambled for. Even during the early stages of the clearance, it was clear that the traditional way of doing Egyptological business was changing. Carnarvon was the last of the rich sponsoring individuals who supported archeologists for a share of the spoils, a practice epitomized by Theodore Davis, the robber baron. The rising tide of Egyptian nationalism, the increasingly scientific approaches of archaeological research, better training of its practitioners, and the spectacular nature of the tomb, as well as changing currents of public opinion, made *partage*, the sharing of the spoils, an anachronism. In the end, Carnarvon's heirs received some reimbursement for the Fifth Earl's sponsorship but none of the loot, almost all of which remained in Egypt, as it should have done.

All pharaohs craved immortality as a fundamental part of their close relationship with the gods. Most of them never achieved any lasting memorial. Robbers looted their sepulchers within a few generations or, if they were lucky, centuries. Ironically, only one pharaoh, one of the least known and most obscure, achieved immortality, and that on a scale unimaginable to those who buried him—Nebkheperure Tutankhamun, the Living Image of Amun. He achieved it because an English aristocrat with a sense of entitlement decided to go digging and laid a successful bet.

"Let Me Tell You a Tale"
A Chapter for Archaeologists

We were looking at a confusion of stone tools from a 5,000-year-old site on the shore of Southern California's Santa Barbara Channel. Knives, scrapers, pounding and grinding stones, and a jumble of waste flakes from tool making lay in piles and rows on the lab table. A few feet away, a second table displayed different fish bones and mollusks heaped on paper plates.

"Typical midden assemblage," remarked Tom, the archaeologist who had dug the site in advance of a housing development. "No burials, which made things easier with the site monitors. But the developer wants more than a technical report. He wants me to write the story of the site for a general audience that he can give to the people who buy his houses, and for publicity. And I want to encourage him, for he's been most cooperative, unlike some of them. But how the hell am I going to make this interesting? I mean, I can describe and analyze everything for archaeologists—but for everyone else?"

He shrugged his shoulders resignedly at the piles of stones. I thought to myself that I have this kind of conversation with a colleague about once a month.

"Tell a story about the site," I replied. "The artifacts and shells tell us about the people who made them, who fished and ate mollusks here 5,000 years ago. Forget the technicalities, they're for the experts. Provided you're accurate and tell the readers at the end of the story where they can find the details, no one's going to mind."

"But how do I start?" Tom asked despairingly. "This is quite unlike an academic paper or a CRM report."

"Write down some questions that will be answered in your story," I replied. "What did the settlement look like? How far offshore, and when, did they catch fish? Why did they collect mollusks? Did they trade any of them? What were environmental conditions like at the time? And why was the site abandoned? If you craft a beginning and an end for your narrative, the rest should fall into place."

Lord and Pharaoh by Brian Fagan,
pp. 141–152. © 2015 Left Coast Press, Inc. All rights reserved.

I left Tom scribbling notes on his computer. During the weeks that followed, I read draft after draft for him, pulling sentences and words apart, asking awkward questions, and trying to prevent him from being too technical. If I were asked to sum up the experience, and in the end the developer was pleased with the story, I would quietly utter, probably to the horror of my colleagues: "Forget the academics, just write an interesting story. And just be accurate."

Translating the Past for All of Us

All archaeologists have the problem of translating their stones and bones, or other finds, into an interesting story for a broad audience. Even finds as spectacular as those from Tutankhamun's tomb are a challenge to turn from museum pieces into the flesh and blood King T. There's a another problem, too. We archaeologists write our stories for fellow academics. They place them in theoretical contexts and describe technical methods that are of little or no interest to a more general audience. Nor are such readers interested in the shortcomings of earlier research, archaeology, like all science, being a cumulative discipline. Changing hypotheses about, say, the death of Tutankhamun or the collapse of Maya civilization are one thing. Debates about cultural processes are another. Few of us write habitually for general audiences or are comfortable doing so. So this chapter is targeted at the practicing archaeologist more than the lay reader—to show how I tried to make an interesting story from a diverse and often dauntingly specialized range of sources. Even if you're not a practicing archaeologist, this chapter may help you to understand the important link between what archaeologists find and the stories about the past that they tell.

Archaeology has long fascinated people everywhere, especially when we make spectacular discoveries, preferably laden with gold. We are seen as adventurous explorers, somewhat like Hollywood's Indiana Jones. But, as we all know, most of our work is slow moving, monotonous, and concerned with the definitely unspectacular. Nevertheless, much of our research is of great importance to our own world, however seemingly trivial. It brings important lessons from the past to the present. We provide insights into societies whose unwritten history is lost, about brilliant environmental adaptations to climate changes large and small, and about the changing roles of men and women in ancient societies—to mention only a few examples.

Over the past quarter century, archaeologists have realized that communicating with broader audiences, with stakeholders in the past, whoever they are, is central to their work and to the survival of archaeology as a way of understanding humanity. What are commonly termed Community Archaeology and Public Archaeology have become flourishing subfields in recent years. In an era of government funding cutbacks and shrinking budgets, we are struggling to convince both policy makers and the wider public that archaeology is worth the expense. We're frantically grappling with the big question of how to take our work—prosaic stone artifacts, animal bones, soil residues, clay potsherds, and all the unspectacular detritus of ancient lives—and turn it into stories about people of the past. And we have to achieve this within the boundaries set by our finds and what we know about them from science. That is what I advised Tom (and many others) to do and what I have tried to achieve here.

To demonstrate this as a form of case study in writing archaeology, I picked a famous story. The discovery of Tutankhamun's tomb is arguably the most published story about archaeology in the world. Howard Carter's words, "It is wonderful," often shortened to "wonderful things," resonate through classrooms across the world. The pharaoh's golden mask has become an icon for archaeology and Ancient Egypt. One would have thought that practically everything that could be said or written about Carter, his patron Lord Carnarvon, and their extraordinary find in the Valley of the Kings has been uttered or committed to paper by now. However, with only a few years to go before the centenary of that dramatic moment on November 25 1922, we need to brace ourselves for an inevitable cascade of yet more books on the subject. So the challenge was to write something different, something that turned our carefully researched historical and archaeological information about Lord Carnarvon and Pharaoh Tutankhamen into a set of parallel biographies. Here's how I set about it.

Developing the Idea amid a Saga of Sources

I intended originally to write a story about Lord Carnarvon. There were two excellent biographies of Carter, which drew on copious archaeological and nonarchaeological sources. We know just about as much about Carter as he did himself. The Fifth Earl of Carnarvon, Porchy if you will, is another matter. For such a grandee, he was a remarkably shadowy figure. By all accounts, he was a quiet man, even self-effacing, which titillated my interest in him. The idea seemed intriguing, but I had to face a dilemma that confronts everyone who writes about people of the past, be they British aristocrats or anonymous Southern California fisherfolk of 5,000 years ago. How does one burrow into a person's life and create their biography? The more I read about Carnarvon, the more interesting he became. I soon discovered that much of his correspondence had been destroyed during World War II, which made it hard to get close to him. I also realized that I had neither the patience nor the talent to write a comprehensive life, if such a thing was even possible given the paucity of sources. But there was more than enough to make him a prominent part of the Tutankhamun story in ways that had not been done before. His early life provided a possible story line. He became addicted to gambling on the ponies as a teenager. Did he embark on the Tutankhamun project as a high-stakes gamble? The idea seemed intriguing.

When I sent samples of the Carnarvon story to Mitch Allen, my editorial guru for this project, he urged me to step back and introduce the Tutankhamun story as part of the broader tapestry of early Egyptology. As archaeologists all know, the context of any find, any story is crucial. This struck me as good sense, for a biography, or even a narrative, without a broader perspective often misses the point. So I decided to start with the Emperor Napoléon and my old friend Giovanni Belzoni, whom I had written about extensively many years ago in another book, *The Rape of the Nile.** To start in the early 1800s would provide a nice chronological gradient for the book that would end about a century later.

The sources on Belzoni and Napoléon were, of course, entirely historical. The former wrote his own account of his adventurers, a rough-and-ready book but priceless in that it gives his experiences a wonderful immediacy. Such immediacy, also found in Howard Carter's mesmerizing description of Tutankhamun's sepulcher, made fleshing out the introductory chapters much easier. Belzoni's account of mummy hunting in the Theban Necropolis is one of the vivid classics of archaeological discovery. "I sunk altogether among the broken mummies, with a crash of bones, rags, and wooden cases, which raised such a dust as kept me motionless for a quarter of an hour."[1] It is almost as if you are there. Immediacy, telling quotes, personal experiences: as much as was practicable, I went back to the original writings of Belzoni and his successors. They were eyewitnesses, participants in the unfolding story.

I knew, also, that my potential readers knew little or nothing about the geography and history of nineteenth-century Egypt. The country was a remote backwater until the opening of the Suez Canal in 1869. I had to immerse myself in the turbulent political developments of the day, which led to a British and French presence and greater political stability after 1882. This was when the tourists arrived in force, thanks to steamships, a constant stream of travelers journeying to and from the British Raj in India, and the Nile's warm, dry winter climate. What was it like traveling up and down the river in the late nineteenth century? By the 1890s Egypt had become a fashionable winter destination for affluent travelers and those with weak lungs—like Lord Carnarvon. Where did they stay? How did they occupy their time? I discovered Victorian guidebooks and Thomas Cook with his Nile tours, learned about Shepheard's Hotel in Cairo and its upstream equivalent, the Winter Palace in Luxor. The literature— when it was readable—was rich, diffuse, and a revealing portrait of a long-vanished world. Victorian travelogues tend to be crushingly dull and, in the case of Egypt, often overladen with Scripture and the tale of Moses. Fortunately, there were exceptions, notably *A Thousand Miles up the Nile* published by the romantic novelist Amelia Edwards in 1877. She traveled the river in a *dahabiyyah* and spent the rest of her life writing passionately about the destruction of Ancient Egypt.

Then there were the Egyptologists, who were the archaeological backdrop to Carnarvon's decision to go digging. They were the lesser characters in my story, passing in and out of the narrative and then reappearing in a confusing mélange of contrasting personalities. The French Antiquities Director Gaston Maspero presided over ar-

*References to books mentioned in this chapter, unless quoted from, will be found in the Guide to Further Reading.

chaeologists, their sponsors, and their concessions. We know of his doings from his correspondence and multifarious dealings with such individuals as the eloquent and opinionated Arthur Weigall, the epigrapher Alan Gardiner, the archaeologist Arthur Mace, and others. Their different characters placed the discoveries in human contexts. For instance, Mace was clearly an important player at tomb clearance time and is the least known. He had once participated in a desert excavation where a grand piano arrived by camel. Here he came across as a calm, patient, and observant figure but not the stuff of vivid narrative. Again, the sources were diffuse, a mixture of books and articles published by the characters themselves, telling details culled from biographies of Carter and others, and occasionally archives or newspaper stories. Then there was the flamboyant and ruthless Theodore Davis, an American lawyer whom one can safely call a robber baron, who developed an enthusiasm for Egyptology and embarked on a systematic investigation of the Valley of the Kings at the turn of the twentieth century. Here I was lucky, for John M. Adams's recently published *Theodore Davis's Gilded Age in the Valley of the Kings* (2013) filled a huge gap in my cast of characters, the first definitive biography of Davis to cover his Egyptological adventures.

To summarize, here's a list of some of the major sources that I used to write the story:

Notes taken on several occasions when I visited the major sites in the book, also the tomb as well as the Cairo Museum.

Notes taken when visiting Tutankhamun exhibits in the United Kingdom and the United States, which, of course covered artifacts.

General books on Ancient Egypt and the Valley of the Kings, also Tutankhamun's tomb. These included lavishly illustrated volumes which gave me an additional visual impression of the artifacts.

Biographies of Howard Carter and, when available, other figures.

BBC and other TV programs—superficial but good for background.

The World Wide Web in all its glorious (and sometimes inaccurate) diversity. The translations of Egyptian and classical texts were especially useful. So was Wikipedia.

Conversations with Egyptologists with first-hand experience of the Valley of the Kings and El-Amarna.

Major academic and more general studies of the Amarna pharaohs and their reigns, including academic literature.

Archives in such institutions as the Griffith Institute at Oxford University, the Metropolitan Museum of Fine Art, New York, and the British Museum, consulted through biographers for the most part.

Discussions with fellow (nonarchaeological) writers, who critiqued the manuscript.

The germ of a background story seemed to be taking hold, with ample historical sources to create a rich and, I hope, entertaining narrative about the early development of Egyptology and Carnarvon's role in it. I drafted an outline that began with Napoléon and culminated in the discovery of Tutankhamun's tomb. The story focused on Carnarvon as a major player in a remarkable partnership, which began when the Earl asked Maspero for expert help after digging alone in 1907–1908. His new colleague was Howard Carter, who was convinced that the tomb of Tutankhamun awaited discovery in the Valley of the Kings. Their early work together is little known outside the narrow circles of Egyptology, so this was an obvious starting point, given their monograph on their Theban Necropolis excavations, published in 1912. The rest of the story is familiar to anyone with even a vague interest in archaeology, so I was able to draw on copious sources.

I quickly realized that Carnarvon's early life might hold some clues about his apparent enthusiasm for Egyptology. The issue of sources arose at once. I searched high and low and came across two self-published books by William Cross. His *Lordy* (2012) describes the Earl's youth, and *The Life and Secrets of Almina Carnarvon* (2011) takes up the story after his marriage. Both were useful sources, for Cross has combed the accessible archives and provides year-by-year summaries of the Carnarvons' activities during the years leading up to the discovery. But the interpretations would obviously be mine and many of the small details in these sources were obviously irrelevant to my broad-brushed and necessarily superficial narrative.

As I unpacked Carnarvon's life, I found myself returning again and again to Tutankhamun. Everyone wrote that he was a little-known, obscure ruler, who died in his teens. There was, of course, plenty on DNA analyses, on the research to establish his cause of death, speculation about chariot accidents and so on—stuff that makes good newspaper headlines—but almost nothing on Tutankhamun as a person, or about his reign, beyond a common statement that he restored the worship of the sun god Amun and rejected his father's deity, Aten, the solar disk. So I delved into the arcane reaches of the more specialist literature, notably Aidan Dodson's meticulously researched *Amarna Sunset* (2009), where I discovered enough to flesh out at least an outline of the king's life. Dodson dealt with political events, with personalities, genealogies, and architectural achievements, with inscriptions and edicts. This was the point at which I decided to use the artifacts from the sepulcher as an archive. I was not alone in having done this. Another Egyptologist, Charlotte Booth, had explored this avenue of inquiry for *The Boy behind the Mask* (2007). Her work originated in a study day on Tutankhamun when she realized she wanted to do more than show pictures of the artifacts in the tomb. Her account is more complete than mine, covers some of the same ground, but is slightly more focused on the king's personality and gives a rich background to his life.

I think it was when I learned that both men had died as a result of poor health and mosquito bites that I decided on a bold, perhaps rash, step—to write two biographies in parallel instead of just one. Carnarvon was a known historical figure, whose encounter with the pharaoh was the result of a bold and expensive gamble that paid off, at least in part. In Tutankhamun's case, I faced one of the archaeologist's perennial challenges head on. How do you create a biography of a long dead Egyptian king from artifacts and a palimpsest of inscriptions and architectural clues?

Archaeology, architecture, epigraphy, inscriptions, books by eyewitnesses, archival sources: the raw material was rich and challenging. Weaving a coherent narrative from this multidisciplinary tapestry required careful attention to the themes of the story.

Themes and Outline

I realized from the beginning that this was not a story about artifacts from the pharaoh's tomb but about people. I had decided on two biographies instead, running in parallel because of the striking amount the two men had in common, despite the huge chronological gap between them. Neither enjoyed robust health. Both lived out their early lives in virtual isolation, far removed from the real world. Both were born into situations of remarkable privilege, which gave them a strong sense of entitlement. Tutankhamun didn't live long enough to make full use of his entitlement. Carnarvon used it unashamedly and would never have encountered the pharaoh if he had not. Both became angry when frustrated in their youth; each enjoyed hunting and horses, in the case of the pharaoh chariotry. And, unexpectedly, both died from infections triggered by mosquito bites.

Here, then, were some common threads. But it was Carnarvon's addiction to gambling on racehorses that gave me a driving theme for the discovery, for his taking up Egyptology in the first place. After all, who has not dreamed of finding a gold-laden pharaoh's sepulcher? Here was a rare example of someone who actually lived his or her ambitious dream. There were other themes and undercurrents, too—Carnarvon and Carter's unlikely friendship, the skill with which Ay and Horemheb controlled their pharaoh, the tragic, controversial story of Tutankhamun's queen. Then there was the changing face of Egyptology, from a discipline sponsored by wealthy individuals employing archaeologists, to a new world where Egypt called the shots.

Thinking about the themes generated a four-page, double-spaced outline. Each chapter listed the topics that it would cover, also the linkages between them. This gave a broad overview of the story sufficient to keep me on track. It also gave me the flexibility to deviate from the main themes, to move things around freely, and to follow my nose when writing, an important consideration with narrative of any kind.

The outline fell together easily, largely because the story is chronological. I decided on two chapters to bring the story from General Napoléon to the diggings of Theodore Davis over the turn of the twentieth century. That would get me to the point where I could start the two biographies that would carry the rest of the story. I also made a decision early on to alternate between Tutankhamun and Carnarvon so that both men's early lives followed one upon the other as a way of highlighting the broad similarities in their early lives. This seemed to work well, so I continued the alternation right through the outline, up to the point when the pharaoh died. Thereafter, the story was Carnarvon's alone. In retrospect, I made very few changes to the outline as I wrote.

The Issue of Genre

When contemplating the genre to adopt, I remembered the conversation I had with Tom, and before him with many others. How do you make the past, chronicled from artifacts, food residues, and all the detritus of ancient human behavior, of interest to nonarchaeologists? I had one advantage here. I was writing about a world famous discovery, not the inhabitants of an obscure shell midden. Even so, the challenge was identical—to make people come alive for the reader, whether an English aristocrat of a century ago or an Egyptian pharaoh. The raw material at my disposal was abundant, detailed, and much picked over by experts. This situation brought up the issue of the approach to writing the story, the genre, or style, if you will, to the foreground from the very beginning.

This book is serious nonfiction, but nonfiction aimed at a very broad audience. I rejected several styles at once, notably that of standing over the characters' shoulders and watching them develop and resolve agreements and disagreements like a game of tennis. This would never work when one is writing at a distance of a hundred years, or three thousand. Nor was this a piece of profoundly evocative nonfiction, where literary artifices and flowery description carry the reader into the past as the characters saw it. I realized that this was a story of two men's lives, each very different, that could be told only from an outsider's relatively neutral perspective. This goal was hard to achieve, unless one attempted to develop the characters of the participants without overdoing it.

I've spent a lifetime writing about archaeology for general audiences. Most of the time, I've written books about subjects in which I have no specialist expertise whatsoever—and this in an academic and archaeological world that is ever more technical and specialized. *Lord and Pharaoh* is a case in point, which will resonate with anyone who has ventured outside the narrow confines of their specialty. My knowledge of Egyptology is at best superficial, my fluency in hieroglyphs nonexistent. On the plus side, I've visited Egypt several times and am familiar with the major sites, having even been locked by accident in a royal tomb—in the dark, as I described in Chapter 1. I know the major artifacts pretty well and have enough superficial knowledge to be able to converse moderately intelligently with an Egyptologist. Over the years, I've talked to dozens of them and received invaluable advice. Despite these plusses, I embarked on *Lord* with considerable trepidation, born from years of academic life, of peer review, and an ingrained fear of stepping outside one's intellectual comfort zone. At this point in my career, I branch out with much more confidence than I used to, having learned that it is far less daunting than one might think—provided one pays careful attention to accuracy.

I'm paranoid about correctness. One's general readers assume it. Colleagues expect it. It's also an obligation to those whom one writes about, dead or living. From the perspective of this book, precision had to be balanced against the reality of Egyptology, which is now a mature, if narrow, specialty. The literature that I read defined my familiarity with the subject. So did conversations with colleagues and, of course, my own first-hand experience of the Theban Necropolis and the Valley of the Kings. I think I have written a pretty accurate story, despite the huge gaps in our knowledge. Having said that, I should confess that this is about the most speculative book on the past I've ever written.

Through these pages, I skated delicately and repeatedly on knife-edges of controversy, many of them unresolved for generations. How does one handle them in a book for a general audience, when the different positions depend on often obscure evidence of at most marginal interest to anyone but a participant? Did, for instance, Tutankhamun's widow actually write to the Hittite king begging him for a husband? Was other correspondence between the same monarch and the Egyptian pharaoh recorded in the Amarna tablets addressed to Tutankhamun or to his father? Then there's the arcane issue of coregencies during Akhenaten's reign as well as Tutankhamun's. Of all the problems that daunt prospective archaeological writers, the issue of controversies is the most intractable. My strategy is very simple. I boldly stake out a position but make careful note of competing ideas, so that no one can accuse me of ignoring them. A case in point involves the Amarna Tablets and the letter written to the Hittite king by Tutankhamun's widow. The tablets document the correspondence, but who are the people referred to in the cuneiform record? In this case, was the Nipkhururiya referred to on the tablet actually the dead pharaoh? And was the "king's wife" in fact Queen Akhesenamun? Since Tutankhamun's prename was Nipkhururiya, I believed (as do many Egyptologists) that the case was a strong one. But in my note to the controversy (Chapter 9, note 6), I mentioned and briefly discussed the other possible explanation. My critics can remark that I am wrong or that they disagree with me, but they certainly cannot accuse me of being unaware of alternative hypotheses and keeping the reader in ignorance of them. I've done this on several occasions in these pages. I may be proven wrong, but I've tried to cut through the ambiguities of the relevant scholarship. It's worth pointing out that there will probably never be a last word on many of the events involving Tutankhamun.

Lord and Pharaoh is unique among my books about the past in that I've used dialogue. To many academics and nonfiction writers, this is a no-no. But fictional dialogue among real historical characters is a literary device that breaks up the narrative for the reader. One can use it to set up conflict and dialectics more graphically than with standard text. For example, I used it to dramatize the angry exchange between Ay and Tutankhamun over the young pharaoh going to war. In this case, and sparingly elsewhere, I felt that conversation invented by me added useful dimensions to the narrative, provided that the dialogue was credible enough that it might have actually happened. Of course, I, as the author, wasn't present when the characters spoke, nor did I write the dialogue in New Kingdom Egyptian, but the points I have them make are valid ones. Numerous historical novelists put words into the mouths of historical figures. Mary Renault's classic account of Theseus and the legend of the Minotaur, *The King Must Die*, is a wonderful example.

Assembling the Jigsaw

Writing this book has been a fascinating exercise in storytelling. It involved not only complex research and a wide diversity of sources but also strategies that come from the world of writers rather than archaeologists. The nub of the problem here, as it is with any popular archaeological writing, is integrating highly technical analyses of artifacts, slow-moving excavations, and day after day of monotonous rubble clearance into the narrative. In the case of *Lord and Pharaoh*, there was the Downton Abbey phenomenon—it is nothing else. The Abbey could be a hook to attract readers to the real stories that emanated from Highclere Castle, but I had to be careful to keep the Abbey and its denizens in the background, for the TV characters bear no substantive relevance to the Carnarvon story. Regardless of the subject matter, one must contextualize one's key figures, even if these figures are artifacts, into a broader milieu—such as the artistic achievements of Cro-Magnons, the ritual beliefs associated with a Maya conch trumpet, or the sound effects echoing through the passages at the temple of Chavín de Huantar in highland Peru. In the case of Carnarvon and Tutankhamun, there were two milieus—that of the Earl, a classic nineteenth-century landowner and aristocrat, and Tutankhamun, who during his reign *was* Egypt, the intermediary between his people and Amun.

Puzzling out how to do this, how to meld the two milieus, took hours of conversation with fellow writers, none of whom knew anything about archaeology. They write fiction and nonfiction but insisted that I examine the characters of the two men. Ultimately, the solution was two parallel biographies, one of an Englishman, the other of an Egyptian king. Once this strategy fell into place, the telling of the story proved relatively straightforward—writing the finds in the royal tombs into the narratives, adding Giovanni Belzoni and the Deir el-Bahari cache, *provided* I kept a clear eye on the general thrust of the narrative and the chronological gradient for the story, which everyone agreed was essential. If there's single lesson from writing *Lord and Pharaoh* it is that one must let the characters have a voice, be they artifacts, a temple, or once-living characters. Peoples' own words speak volumes, so I used quotes from people's writings judiciously. Portraits and other artworks can be eloquent witnesses, too. Ay performing the Opening of the Mouth ceremony on the walls of Tutankhamun's burial chamber speaks volumes about the politics of succession and adds telling background to the controversies over who was the next pharaoh. Artifacts were powerful storytellers, especially such finds as the pharaoh's writing implements and his walking sticks. Let no one say that one cannot reconstruct a convincing and accurate archaeological story from artifacts alone. One can do it with the seemingly most prosaic objects.

As when excavating and analyzing a site, I thought of the story in these pages as an intricate jigsaw puzzle of small pieces, which, when fitted together, formed a coherent narrative. The analogy is appropriate, because we archaeologists spend our careers putting together ancient jigsaw puzzles. There was no particular magic in writing the story once the pieces came together. I asked questions of the material, a technique that works well. Where does, say, a grinding stone and pounder fit into your portrait of a society? What does it tell us about male and female roles? As far as style was concerned, I followed the sage advice of Strunk and Wagnall's *Elements of Style*: "Vigorous writing is concise. A statement should contain no unnecessary words, a paragraph no unnecessary sentences."[2] Writing about the past from one's finds comes down to identifying the people behind them and making them come alive. No one says it's easy, but it can be done, as Howard Carter did with Tutankhamun's sepulcher: "The very air you breathe, unchanged through the centuries, you share with those who laid the mummy to rest. Time is annihilated by little intimate details such as these, and you feel an intruder."[3] Enough said.

A Chronological Framework of Egypt

Any chronology of Ancient Egypt and its pharaohs is an academic minefield, which makes it near impossible to pin down the regnal dates of individual rulers. The outline that follows is a general framework to accompany the text and is the chronology I have generally adhered to in the book.

Predynastic and Earlier Times — Before 3100 B.C.

A series of Egyptian kingdoms developed out of farming communities, perhaps in part as a result of in-migration of cattle people from the drying Sahara Desert.

Archaic (Early Dynastic) Period — ca. 3100 B.C.–2686 B.C.

Lower and Upper Egypt (The Two Lands) were unified, perhaps by the pharaoh Narmer in about 3100 B.C. The centuries that followed saw the consolidation of pharaonic rule: Dynasties I–III.

Old Kingdom — 2686 B.C.–2181 B.C.

Five centuries of despotic rule and prosperity. This was the time when the pharaohs were buried under pyramids: Dynasties IV–VI.

First Intermediate Period — 2181 B.C.–2160 B.C.

A time of fragmentation and confusion, and persistent drought, that ended with Thebes asserting control over a reunited state: Dynasties VII–XI.

Middle Kingdom — 1225 B.C.–1773 B.C.

A period of strong pharaohs and great prosperity following reunification: Dynasties XII–XIII.

Second Intermediate Period — 1773 B.C.–1550 B.C.

Hyksos invaders from Asia rule the Delta. Egypt effectively becomes two kingdoms, the second based on Thebes in Upper Egypt: Dynasties XIV–XVII.

New Kingdom — 1550 B.C.–1070 B.C.

Three dynasties of pharaohs presided over an increasingly militaristic Egypt, at the height of its influence as an international power.

XVIII Dynasty   ca. 1550–1295 (including Tutankhamun)
XIX Dynasty   1295–1186
XX Dynasty   1186–1070

Late Period — 1070 B.C.–1030 B.C.

Egypt was a progressively weaker international presence, dominated at different times by Nubian rulers, the Assyrians, Alexander the Great, Persians, and the Ptolemies, pharaohs of Greek origin. The center of political gravity moved progressively northward to the Nile Delta: Dynasties XXI–XXXIII.

Roman Times — 30 B.C. to 6th century A.D.

Egypt became a major grain producer for Rome after Mark Anthony's conquest in 30 B.C. and the wealthiest province of the Empire. It became a Christian province in 33 A.D., after which most pharaonic traditions began to vanish. When the Empire split, Egypt became part of the Byzantine/Eastern Roman Empire based on Constantinople.

Islamic Egypt — 639 A.D.–1250

Egypt was conquered by Amr Ibn Al-Aas, who captured Alexandria in 641. It became an Islamic country and the base for the Arab conquest of North Africa. The Arabs remained in control of Egypt until it came under the control of the Mamluks.

Mamluk Egypt — 1250-1517

Mamluk horsemen from the Eurasian steppes were the backbone of the Egyptian army. They seized power in 1250 but were conquered by the Ottomans in 1517.

Ottoman Egypt — 1517-1867

Following the defeat of the Mamluks by the Ottoman Empire, based in Constantinople, the country became an Ottoman province but was still ruled by Mamluks, as Ottoman vassals. A constant struggle for independence ensued.

Napoléon Bonaparte Invades Egypt — 1798-1801

The French invasion of Egypt and the arrival of the savants (see Chapter 1).

Muhammed Ali and His Dynasty — 1805-1882

Muhammed Ali, an Albanian commander in the Ottoman army, became governor, then Pasha of Egypt, eliminating the Mamluks and establishing Egypt as a regional power. He laid the foundations of the modern Egyptian state. His successors after his death in 1848 included Ismail the Magnificent, who supported the building of the Suez Canal, opened in 1867. Ismail drove Egypt into bankruptcy, paving the way for foreign intervention to control the country's debt.

Egypt and the British — 1882-1956

Between 1882 and 1956, British soldiers were stationed in Egypt. The country was under a nominal protectorate after its finances were taken over. The late nineteenth and early twentieth centuries witnessed an explosion in international tourism and the first large scale archaeological expeditions along the Nile. Egypt became an independent protectorate in 1922 but was effectively dominated by the British, who controlled the Suez Canal.

Egyptian Independence — (1952-   )

Egypt declared itself independent of Britain in 1952 and nationalized the Suez Canal two years later, a development that triggered the Suez Crisis of 1956, when Britain, France, and Israel invaded the country and seized the canal. International pressure forced them to withdraw. Egypt has been an independent republic ever since.

A Short Guide to the Pharaohs of the XVIII to XX Dynasties Mentioned in the Narrative

Dates are for their reigns (regnal dates). The tomb numbers given for each pharaoh are those commonly used by Egyptologists and are also used in the text.

XVII Dynasty

- **Khamose (ca. 1555–1550 B.C.) (tomb location unknown)**

Brother of his successor Ahmose. He ruled over Upper Egypt and conquered the Hyksos. His conquests appear on the Carnarvon Tablet, his reign lasting three to five years.

XVIII Dynasty

Some early XVIII Dynasty pharaohs:

- **Ahmose (1570–1546 B.C.) (tomb location unknown)**

The first XVIII Dynasty pharaoh. Known as The Liberator, Ahmose reunified Egypt after the Hyksos invasions and consolidated Egypt's boundaries.

- **Amenhotep I (1551–1524 B.C.) (tomb location unknown ?KV 39)**

Said to be the first pharaoh buried in the Valley of the Kings, Amenhotep I is an obscure figure. He is known to have campaigned successfully in Nubia.

- **Tuthmosis I (1524–1518) (tomb ?KV 20, later KV 38?)**

A military man, Tuthmosis I occupied his short reign with successful campaigns against the Nubians and restored Karnak to its former glory.

Now a continual sequence:

- **Queen Hatshepsut (1498–1483 B.C.) (tomb KV 20)**

Egypt's first female pharaoh, she is famous for her trading expeditions, especially down the Red Sea to the Land of Punt, probably northern Somalia or Djibuti.

- **Tuthmosis III (1504–1450 B.C.) (tomb KV 34)**

An expert military man, he campaigned successfully in the Levant seventeen times, inscribing some of his victories on the walls of the sanctuary at Karnak. His reign was remarkable for its opulence.

- **Amenhotep II (1453–1419 B.C.) (tomb KV 35)**

A successful military man, Amenhotep II suppressed rebellions among the eastern Mediterranean sea ports and campaigned successfully in Nubia. His Valley tomb was later used by the necropolis priests to hide other royal mummies.

- **Tuthmosis IV (1419–1386 B.C.) (tomb KV 43)**

This little-known ruler is best known for an inscription recording how he allegedly cleared sand from the Sphinx at Giza and became pharaoh. He may have undertaken military campaigns in Syria.

- **Amenhotep III (1386–1349 B.C.) (tomb KV 22)**

Amenhotep III presided over a peaceful and prosperous Egypt, also a peak of artistic achievement. His chief wife was Tiye (or Tiy), daughter of the courtier Yuya and his wife Tuya.

- **Akhenaten (1351–1334 B.C.) (tomb location unknown)**

The so-called heretic pharaoh, who banished the worship of Amun in favor of the sun disk, the Aten. He moved the royal capital to Akhetaten (modern-day El-Amarna), downstream of Thebes. Tutankhamun's father (see Chapter 3).

- **Smenkhkare (1336–1334 B.C.) (?tomb KV 55)**

Probably a younger brother of Akhenaten, his short reign was probably a coregency with his brother. His wife was Merytaten, who predeceased him. Her sister, Ankhesen-paaten (later Ankhesenamun), married Tutankhaten (Tutankhamun).

- **Tutankhaten/Tutankhamun (1334–1325 B.C.) (tomb KV 62)**

See relevant chapters.

- **Ay (1325–1321 B.C.) (tomb KV 23)**

Tutankhamun's closest adviser and former military man, who succeeded him. See Chapters 5, 7, and 9.

- **Horemheb (1321–1293 B.C.) (tomb KV 57)**

A military man who became King's Deputy under Tutankhamun, then pharaoh after Ay. See Chapters 7 and 9.

XIX DYNASTY

- **Ramesses I (1293–1291 B.C.) (tomb KV 16)**

A career military officer who became pharaoh after Horemheb and reigned for only two years. Little is known about him.

- **Seti I (1291–1278 B.C.) (tomb KV 17)**

A military man and former vizier, Seti I campaigned against the Syrians and Libyans. His victories are commemorated on the walls of Amun's temple at Karnak. Seti's ambitious building programs included starting the Hypostele Hall at Karnak.

- **Ramesses II (1279–1212 B.C.) (tomb KV 7)**

Ramesses the Great built prodigious numbers of temples, statues, and obelisks, including the Abu Simbel temple in Nubia. In 1275 B.C. he battled the Hittites inconclusively at Kadesh (or Qadesh) in Syria, an engagement he commemorated on the walls of Amun's temples at Karnak, Luxor, and at his mortuary temple. He also constructed a magnificent city at Piramesse ("Domain of Ramesses") in the Delta. Ramesses II died in his early nineties.

- **Merneptah (1212–1202 B.C.) (tomb KV 8)**

Ramesses II's thirteenth son, who crushed rebellion in Syria, ousted invading Libyans, and defeated Nubian rebels during a reign of ten years.

Later XIX Dynasty pharaohs:

- **Seti II (1193–1187 B.C.) (tomb KV 56)**

An obscure pharaoh, husband of Queen Twosret, stepmother of Siptah. His short reign unfolded at a time of serious political upheaval.

- **Siptah (1193–1187 B.C.) (tomb KV 47)**

A short-reigning king, Siptah was the younger son of Seti II. His mummy shows that he had a clubfoot, perhaps as a result of contracting poliomyelitis when young.

XX DYNASTY

- **Ramesses III (1182–1151 B.C.) (tomb KV 11)**

The last of Egypt's great pharaohs ruled when the eastern Mediterranean world was in turmoil. He fought off marauding Libyans twice and defeated the so-called Sea Peoples, who sought to settle in Egypt, on land and sea. He commemorated his victory on the walls of his mortuary temple at Medinet Habu. His tomb is famous for its depictions of blind harpists.

- **Ramesses IX (1126–1108 B.C.) (tomb KV 6)**

He presided over a relatively stable Egypt, when pharaonic power was strongest in the Delta. Power in the south shifted increasingly to the priests of Amun.

- **Ramesses XI (1098–1070 B.C.) (tomb KV 4)**

The last of the XX Dynasty pharaohs, Ramesses XI presided over Egypt at time of chronic instability. He ruled from the Delta, perhaps sharing power with a powerful priest of Amun in Thebes.

Further Reading

A huge literature surrounds Tutankhamun and the discovery of his tomb. The Further Reading section that follows is but a small sample of the popular and specialist articles and books I consulted to write this book. Most contain excellent bibliographies for those who wish to delve deeper into the subject.

General Works

Nicholas Reeves, *The Complete Tutankhamun* (London and New York: Thames and Hudson, 1990), is a comprehensive description of the tomb and provides general background. The illustrations are superb. For a dazzling excursion through the artifacts in the tomb, look no farther than T. G. H. James, *Tutankhamun: The Eternal Splendor of the Boy Pharaoh* (London and New York: Tauris Park Books, 2000). The illustrations take your breath away. Nicholas Reeves and Richard H. Wilkinson, *The Complete Valley of the Kings* (London and New York: Thames and Hudson, 1996), tell you all you want to know about the Valley and more. Peter Clayton's *Chronicle of the Pharaohs* (London and New York: Thames and Hudson, 1994) is an excellent basic source on Egypt's kings. Toby Wilkinson, *The Rise and Fall of Ancient Egypt* (New York: Random House, 2010), is a compelling and intelligent overview of Ancient Egyptian civilization for the general reader.

Chapter 1: A Valley of Pharaohs

Much of the material in this chapter is based on the *Complete Valley of the Kings*, referred to under General Works. My *The Rape of the Nile*, 3rd ed. (Boulder, CO: Westview Press, 2004) summarizes the early history of tomb robbing and Egyptology. Stanley Mayes, *The Great Belzoni* (New York: Tauris Parke, reprinted 2003), and Ivor Nöel Hume, *Belzoni: The Giant Archaeologists Love to Hate* (Charlotteville: Univer-

Lord and Pharaoh by Brian Fagan,
pp. 161–164. © 2015 Left Coast Press, Inc. All rights reserved.

sity of Virginia Press, 2011), cover this remarkable figure thoroughly. Decipherment: Andrew Robinson, *Cracking the Egyptian Code: The Revolutionary Life of Jean-François Champollion* (New York: Oxford University Press, 2012). John Gardner Wilkinson: Jason Thompson, *John Gardner Wilkinson and His Circle* (Austin: University of Texas Press, 2010).

Chapter 2: Discoveries of a Self-Made Man

The flamboyant and hard driving Theodore Davis has become a background figure, overshadowed as his work was by Tutankhamun. John M. Adams, *Theodore Davis's Gilded Age in the Valley of the Kings* (New York: St. Martin's Press, 2013), sets the record straight admirably in an entertaining biography. For details of the burials he discovered over and above this source, see *Complete Valley of the Kings* cited under General Works. The Adams volume does much to describe the supporting cast of archaeologists behind the Davis excavations. Howard Carter is, of course, one of the best known of all archaeologists and has been extensively biographized, notably by H. G. F. Winstone, *Howard Carter and the Discovery of the Tomb of Tutankhamun*, rev. ed. (London: Barzan Books, 2007), and T. G. H. James, *Howard Carter: The Path to Tutankhamun*, rev ed. (London and New York: Tauris Books, 2001). James's book is truly definitive.

Chapter 3: "Effective for Aten"

The literature on Akhenaten is enormous. Barry Kemp, *The City of Akhenaten and Nefertiti: Amarna and Its People* (London and New York: Thames and Hudson, 2012) is the fundamental source on his city. Aidan Dodson's *Amarna Sunrise* (Cairo: American University in Cairo Press, 2009) is a closely argued account of the events in this chapter, based on an intricate palimpsest of inscriptions, archaeological finds, and art objects. This is professional Egyptology at its best and well worth a nonspecialist's perusal. Garry J. Shaw, *The Pharaoh: Life at Court and on Campaign* (London and New York: Thames and Hudson, 2012), is a layperson's guide to royal life and admirable for a beginner (like me). See also Charlotte Booth, *The Boy behind the Mask: Meeting the Real Tutankhamun* (Oxford: Oneworld Publications, 2007).

Chapter 4: A Gambler with Enthusiasms

Lord Carnarvon's early life has only recently been discussed in detail. Many details still remain obscure. William Cross, *Lordy: Tutankhamun's Patron as a Young Man* (Newport, Gwent, South Wales: Book Midden Publishing, 2012), provides a comprehensive, broad-brushed look at this youth. It is useful for its citations of basic sources. A hagiographic account of Lord Carnarvon's life: Winifred, Lady Burghclere, "Biographical Sketch of the Late Lord Carnarvon" appears in Howard Carter and A. C. Mace,

The Tomb of Tut.Ankh.Amen (New York: Cooper Square Publishers, 1963 [reprint]), pp.1–40. Popular books include The Countess of Carnarvon, *Lady Catherine, the Earl, and the Real Downton Abbey* (New York: Broadway Books, 2013), and the same author's *Lady Almina and the Real Downton Abbey: The Lost Legacy of Highclere Castle* (New York: Broadway Books, 2011).

Chapter 5: Tutankhamun the Justified

Aidan Dodson's *Amarna Sunrise*, already cited, and his *Amarna Sunset* (Cairo: American University in Cairo Press, 2009), are fundamental, if intricate, sources for this chapter. So are Barry Kemp, *The City of Akhenaten*, already cited, and Garry J. Shaw's *The Pharaoh*, referred to in Chapter 3. Charlotte Booth's *Boy behind the Mask*, cited in Chapter 3, is also useful. T. G. H. James's *Tutankhamun: The Eternal Splendor* provides the illustrations for the artifacts referred to here.

Chapter 6: "The Records of the Past Are Not Ours to Play With"

Amelia Edwards, *A Thousand Miles up the Nile* (London: Longmans Green, 1877), provides an evocative account of Victorian tourism along the Nile. Andrew Humphreys, *Grand Hotels of Egypt in the Golden Age of Travel* (Cairo: American University in Cairo Press, 2011), describes the bustling hotels and social life of Egyptian winters. Lord Carnarvon and Howard Carter, *Five Years Exploration at Thebes: A Record of Work Done 1907–1911* (London: Oxford University Press, 1912), reports on Carnarvon's early necropolis work. Arthur Weigall, *Tutankhamen and Other Essays* (Port Washington, NY: Kennikat Press, 1970, reprint of 1923 edition), makes for good reading.

Chapter 7: Restorer of Amun

The best source on Tutankhamun's reign is Aidan Dodson's *Amarna Sunset* (Cairo: American University in Cairo Press, 2009), which discusses the many controversies surrounding the subject. William Moran's *The Amarna Letters* (Baltimore: Johns Hopkins University Press, 2000) is a fascinating portrait of XVIII Dynasty diplomacy. Once again, Garry J. Shaw's *The Pharaoh* and Charlotte Booth's *The Boy behind the Golden Mask*, both cited earlier, are useful sources.

Chapter 8: The Search Narrows

Lord Carnarvon and Howard Carter, *Five Years Exploration*, is a primary source on the two men's first excavations together. For the events leading up to the discovery of the tomb, there is no better synthesis than T. G. H. James, *Howard Carter*. For immediacy and drama, you can do no better than Howard Carter and A. C. Mace, *The Tomb of*

Tut.Ankh.Amen. William Cross's *Almina Carnarvon* covers the facts of the World War I years and Almina's later life.

Chapter 9: Death of a Pharaoh

Again, the best source is Aidan Dodson, *Amarna Sunset* (Cairo: American University in Cairo, 2009), which is particularly good on the Hittite affair. I relied on Garry J. Wills, *The Pharaoh*, for funerary details. Nicholas Reeves, *The Complete Tutankhamun*, is your best guide to the tomb. See also Bob Brier, *The Murder of Tutankhamun* (New York: Berkley Trade, 2005).

Chapter 10: "I Have Got Tutankhamun!"

Ultimately, there is only one guide to the events in this chapter: Howard Carter and A. C. Mace's *The Tomb of Tut.Ankh.Amen* has a wonderful excitement about it that could come only from first-hand experience. Once again, T. G. H. James's *Howard Carter* is a reliable guide to the nuances of the discovery.

Chapter 11: Aftermath

Howard Carter and A. C. Mace's *The Tomb of Tut.Ankh.Amen* and T. G. H. James's *Howard Carter* (Chapters 10 to 12) are your best guides. Howard Carter, *Tut.Ankh. Amen: The Politics of Discovery* (London: Libri Publications, 1998), provides his statement of documents and grievances in full if you wish to visit a dreary controversy of nearly a century ago. For Lord Carnarvon's collection: Nicholas Reeves, *Ancient Egypt at Highclere Castle* (Newbury: Highclere Castle, 1989).

Notes

Front Matter

1. From the Papyrus of Nebseni. British Museum 9,900, sheet 16, E. A. Wallis Budge, Trans., *The Chapters of Coming Forth by Day* (London: Kegan Paul, Trench and Trüber, 1898). Rubric for Chapter CXXI, p. 128. Nebseni was a priest and scribe during the XVIII Dynasty. Little is known about him.

2. Quoted from Judith Robinson, *The Hearsts: An American Dynasty* (San Francisco: Telegraph Hill Press, 1991), p. 325.

Chapter 1

1. This is a generic series of royal names; quoted from http://www.livius.org/pha-phd/pharaoh/pharaoh.htm.

2. Strabo, *Geography*, Book XVII. Horace Leonard Jones, trans. *Strabo's Geography* (Cambridge, MA: Harvard University Press, 1932), Book XVII, Chapter 1, §46. Strabo, a consummate traveler and geographer, was born in Turkey when it was part of the Roman Empire. He wrote his *Geography* during the first century A.D.

3. The Valley of the Kings is an archaeological maze, which confuses even specialists. My description is based on Nicholas Reeves and Richard H. Wilkinson, *The Complete Valley of the Kings* (London and New York: Thames and Hudson,1996), which is the best source for general readers. Information here from Chapter 1.

4. For details of Egypt's pharaohs, see Peter A. Clayton, *Chronicle of the Pharaohs* (London and New York: Thames and Hudson, 1994). This is the best comprehensive summary for lay people and well-illustrated into the bargain.

5. This section is based on my *The Rape of the Nile*, 3rd ed. (Boulder, CO: Westview Press, 2004). Giovanni Belzoni was a remarkable character by any standards, let alone those of the early nineteenth century. At home in a drawing room, on the stage, or in a pyramid or royal tomb, he was a charismatic tomb robber and a consummate showman. A popular, very readable biography: Stanley Mayes, *The Great Belzoni* (New York: Tauris Parke, 2003).

6. Prince Mentuherkhepeshef was a son of Ramesses IX. His tomb has superb paintings depicting an elegantly dressed prince. See Nicholas Reeves and Richard H. Wilkinson, *The Complete Valley*, pp. 170–71.

7. Letter from Walter Scott to the publisher John Murray, May 19, 1820. Quoted from Stanley Mayes, *The Great Belzoni*, p. 253.

8. Champollion was another compelling, if eccentric, character who has been biographized in English only recently. This passage is based on Andrew Robinson's admirable *Cracking the Egyptian Code: The Revolutionary Life of Jean-François Champollion* (New York: Oxford University Press, 2012).

9. John Gardner Wilkinson was a talented artist and a man of many parts, who thoroughly enjoyed himself in Egypt when a young man. My description is based on a definitive biography: Jason Thompson, *John Gardner Wilkinson and His Circle* (Austin, TX: University of Texas Press, 2010). For Wilkinson's take on Egypt, consult his *A Handbook for Travellers in Egypt* (London: John Murray, 1847).

10. Described by Nicholas Reeves and Richard H. Wilkinson, *The Complete Valley*, pp. 194–97.

11. Gaston Maspero with Émile Brugsch, *La Trouvaille de Deir el-Bahari* (Paris, Hachette, 1881), p. 57.

Chapter 2

1. John M. Adams, *Theodore Davis's Gilded Age in the Valley of the Kings* (New York: St. Martin's Press, 2013) is a comprehensive source that I relied on for much of this chapter; quotes from p. 30. Readers interested in Davis's career as a lawyer should consult Adams's book.

2. Quoted by John M. Adams, *Theodore Davis*, p. 313.

3. Flinders Petrie, *Ten Years Digging in Egypt, 1881–1891*, 2nd ed. (London: Religious Tract Society, 1893) provides insights into the crude scientific digging methods of the day. He was a better excavator than most, for he insisted on the importance of the small artifact. E. A. Wallis Budge (1857–1934) was a British Museum official, well known for his popular books on the ancient world. He was also a notoriously unscrupulous collector in Egypt and Mesopotamia.

4. T. G. H. James's *Howard Carter: The Path to Tutankhamun*, rev. ed. (London and New York: Tauris Books, 2001) is a comprehensive source, written by a gifted Egyptologist. This important book is also good on lesser archaeological personalities of the day. Percy Newberry (1869–1949) was a talented artist and botanical expert, who worked on the plant specimens from Tutankhamun's tomb.

5. Elliot Grafton Smith (1871–1937) was an Australian-born British anatomist, who was an expert on the brain and a pioneer in the use of X rays, which he tried on Ancient Egyptian mummies. He was also the creator of a theory of "hyperdiffusionism," a long-discredited hypothesis that "The Children of the Sun," originating in Ancient Egypt, had spread civilization throughout the ancient world.

6. Arthur Weigall (1880–1934) was a well-known archaeological figure in Egypt when working under Gaspar Maspero. He apprenticed under Petrie and developed austere ideas about excavation (see Chapter 6). Socially adept, he later became a gifted London theatrical set designer and a journalist. He was a fluent writer who wrote widely about archaeology and Ancient Egypt, making a nuisance of himself when Carter was working on Tutankhamun's tomb. For a biography, see Julie Hankey, *A Passion for Egypt: Arthur Weigall, Tutankhamun, and the "Curse of the Pharaohs"* (London and New York: Tauris Parke Paperbacks, 2007). Joseph Lindon Smith (1863–1950) was a gifted painter who worked for several Egyptologists, including Theodore Davis, recording wall paintings and artifacts with great skill.

7. John M. Adams, *Theodore Davis*, p. 15.

8. T. G. H. James, *Howard Carter*, Chapter 5, describes this incident in detail.

9. Davis completed his final, lavishly produced report, *The Tombs of Harmhabi and Toutankhamanou* (London: Bristol Classical Press, reprint, 2001) in 1912. The quote comes from the Introduction (p. 3). Ironically, the last page is a color picture of a painting of the blue glazed vase with Tutankhamun's name on it. The vessel was found under a rock in 1905.

Chapter 3

1. Barry Kemp, *The City of Ahkhenaten and Nefertiti: Amarna and Its People* (London and New York: Thames and Hudson, 2012) is the fundamental source on Amarna and forms much of the basis for this chapter. Quote from p. 34. The solar disk, Aten, is sometimes spelled Aton. I have adopted what appears to be the more common spelling, Aten.

2. Peter Clayton, *Chronicle of the Pharaohs* (London and New York: Thames and Hudson, 1994), pp. 120–27, gives a summary of Akhenaten's life.

3. Barry Kemp, *The City*, p. 34.

4. Barry Kemp, *The City*, p. 34.

5. A thorough description of the city based on archaeological research, and drawn on here, appears in Barry Kemp, *The City*, Chapters 3 and 4.

6. Tutankhaten's mother is the subject of unending and unresolved discussion among the experts. Whereas Akhenaten was certainly his father, his mother may have been either Nefertiti, the Great Royal Wife, or Kiya, another wife of the pharaoh. Kiya's origins are obscure, but she might have been a princess named Tadukhepa from Mitanni in Syria. Kiya may have been disgraced and replaced by one of the king's daughters, Meryetaten, who became Akhenaten's Great Wife. To complicate the story, Nefertiti was still alive in Year 16 of the pharaoh's reign. Most experts believe Nefertiti was Tutankhaten's mother, but it should be pointed out that royal princes traditionally married their half-sisters if they were born of a lesser wife to acquire legitimacy if they were likely to become pharaoh. Aidan Dodson has an admirable analysis in his *Amarna Sunrise* (Cairo: American University in Cairo Press, 2014), pp. 130ff. See also the same author's *Amarna Sunset* (Cairo: American University in Cairo Press), Chapters 1 and 2, for background.

7. Maya: Aidan Dodson, *Amarna Sunset*, pp. 48–49.

8. My description of Tutankhamun's infancy and childhood draws heavily on the discussion in Garry J. Shaw, *The Pharaoh: Life at Court and on Campaign* (London and New York: Thames and Hudson, 2012), Chapter 3.

9. Sennedjem: Aidan Dodson, *Amarna Sunset*, pp. 48–49.

10. Gary J. Shaw, *The Pharaoh*, pp. 54–56.

11. Miriam Lichtheim, *Ancient Egyptian* Literature, Vol. 1 (Berkeley and Los Angeles: University of California Press, 1973), pp. 61–80. Quote is from *Maxims of Ptah-hotep*, 6.5.

12. A Middle Kingdom scribe, Khamwee, set down *The Teachings for King Merikare*, but the work is probably much earlier. See http://www.reshafim.org.il/ad/egypt/merikare_papyrus.htm.

13. Barry Kemp, *The City*, pp. 227–29. It's worth noting that bubonic plague has been identified in Egypt as early as 1500 B.C. It may have arrived with black rats, perhaps by indirect sea trade from India.

14. This section is based on Barry Kemp, *The City*, Chapter 3.

15. Barry Kemp, *The City*, Chapter 8.

Chapter 4

1. My account draws heavily on William Cross, *Lordy: Tutankhamun's Patron as a Young Man* (Gwent, South Wales: Book Midden Publishing, 2012), pp. 51ff.

2. Victor Duleep Singh's father, the Maharajah, socialized with King Edward VII and was very well connected. Porchy's Eton days can be found in William Cross, *Lordy,* pp. 102–07; 116–19.

3. William Cross, *Lordy,* pp. 81–03; 98–100.

4. An extended description of these events appears in William Cross, *Lordy,* pp. 130–64.

5. A description of the voyage and of the subsequent elephant hunt appears in Winifred, Lady Burghclere, "Biographical Sketch of the Late Lord Carnarvon." In Howard Carter and A. C. Mace, *The Tomb of Tut.Ankh.Amen* (New York: Cooper Square Publishers, 1963 [reprint]), pp.1–40. Quote from pp. 14–15.

6. My account of Almina is based on William Cross, *The Life and Secrets of Almina Carnarvon* (Gwent, South Wales: William Cross, 2011), pp. 13–22. See also Lady Carnarvon, *Lady Almina and the Real Downton Abbey: The Lost Legacy of Highclere Castle* (New York: Broadway Books, 2011).

7. This all-important encounter has remained in the historical background. See William Cross, *Almina,* pp. 66–67.

8. Lord Cromer was one of Great Britain's great colonial administrators. See Roger Owen, *Lord Cromer: Victorian Imperialist, Edwardian Proconsul* (Oxford: Oxford University Press, 2004).

9. Arthur Weigall, *Glory of the Pharaohs* (London: Putnams, 1923), p. 101.

Chapter 5

1. Aidan Dodson, *Amarna Sunset* (Cairo: American University in Cairo Press, 2009), p. 11. This passage is based on this book, Chapter 1.

2. The *heb-sed* ceremony celebrated the reign of a pharaoh after twenty or thirty years; it was aimed at reinforcing the king's divine powers. Akhenaten celebrated a *heb-sed* after his third year, probably as part of his effort to undermine traditional religious beliefs. Charlotte Booth, *The Boy behind the Mask: Meeting the Real Tutankhamun* (Oxford: Oneworld Publications, 2007), p. 61.

3. T. G. H. James, *Tutankhamun: The Eternal Splendor of the Boy Pharaoh* (London and New York: Tauris Parke Books, 2000) has comprehensive, and spectacular, illustrations of the tomb contents. One cannot do justice to the jewelry in words.

4. John Coleman Darnell and Colleen Manassa, *Tutankhamun's Armies: Battle and Conquest during Egypt's Late Eighteenth Dynasty* (New York: John Wiley, 2007), pp. 77–80. This book is a comprehensive account of armies at the time, drawn on here. There have, of course, been attempts to reconstruct the pharaoh's chariots based on the originals in the tomb.

5. William Moran, *The Amarna Letters* (Baltimore: Johns Hopkins University Press, 2000) is the standard source. For diplomacy, see Aidan Dodson, *Amarna Sunset*, pp. 53–54.

6. Diodorus Siculus was a Greek historian from Sicily, who lived and worked during the first century A.D.; C. H. Oldfather, *Diodorus Siculus: Library of History*, Vol. 1, Books 1–2.34 (Cambridge, MA: Harvard University Press, 1933). Book 1, 70.

7. Aidan Dodson, *Amarna Sunset*, Chapter 6.

8. Barry Kemp, *The City*, pp. 292–96.

9. A non-Egyptologist navigates with caution between the shoals of controversy here. I have taken a rather simple line. Rather than create a lengthy summary, I refer the reader to the comprehensive and well-balanced discussion in Aidan Dodson, *Amarna Sunset*, Chapters 1 and 2.

10. Ankhesenamun is a mystery figure, who stands in the shadows. Little is known about her except for her brief moment in the spotlight when the king died (see Chapter 9). See Charlotte Booth, *The Boy*, pp. 75–83.

11. Pharaonic coronations: Garry J. Shaw, *The Pharaoh*, pp. 64–69.

Chapter 6

1. Arthur Weigall, letter to Francis Griffith, October 1, 1907. Quoted by T. G. H. James, *Howard Carter*, p. 160. For the quote used in the chapter title, see Chapter 4, note 9.

2. Carnarvon's mummified cat is illustrated in Nicholas Reeves, *The Complete Tutankhamun*, p. 44.

2. Brian Fagan, *The Rape*, describes Belzoni's escapades. Quote from p. 97.

3. Ernesto Schiaparelli (1856–1928) was an Italian Egyptologist who found Queen Nefertari's tomb in Deir el-Medina in 1904. He was Director of the Egyptian Museum in Turin and carried out twelve excavation campaigns in Egypt between 1903 and 1920.

4. Amelia Edwards, *A Thousand Miles up the Nile* (London: Longmans Green, 1877) is a classic account of a leisurely tourist trip up the Nile before steamships. Piers Brandon, *Thomas Cook: 150 Years of Popular Tourism* (London: Secker and Warburg, 1991) gives the mass-market perspective.

5. Andrew Humphreys, *Grand Hotels of Egypt in the Golden Age of Travel* (Cairo: American University in Cairo Press, 2011) is an entertaining and informed survey of early twentieth-century Egyptian tourism. Quote from p. 183.

6. Arthur Weigall, letter to Francis Griffith, October 1, 1907. Quoted by T. G. H. James, *Howard Carter*, pp. 160–61.

7. Described in the same letter from Weigall to Francis Griffith, quoted in T. G. H. James, *Howard Carter,* pp. 160–61.

8. Alan H. Gardiner, "The Defeat of the Hyksos by Kamôse: The Carnarvon Tablet, No. 1," *Journal of Egyptian Archaeology* 3 (1916): 95–110.

Chapter 7

1. Quotes from the Restoration Stela in this chapter from J. Bennett, "The Restoration Inscription of Tut'ankhamun," *Journal of Egyptian Archaeology* 25 (1939): 8–25.

2. Aidan Dodson, *Amarna Sunset*, pp. 63–64; 109–10.

3. Aidan Dodson, *Amarna Sunset*, p. 65.

4. Tutankhamun's architectural works: Aidan Dodson, *Amarna Sunset*, pp. 66ff.

5. The passage on Tutankhamun's progress that follows is based on Garry J. Shaw, *The Pharaoh*, pp. 138–42.

6. J. Bennett, "Restoration Inscription", p. 10.

7. Diplomacy: Aidan Dodson, *Amarna Sunset*, Chapter 3, formed the basis for this passage. For the Amarna letters, see William Moran, *The Amarna Letters* (Baltimore: Johns Hopkins University Press, 2000).

8. William Moran, *Amarna Letters*, p. 41.

9. Garry J. Shaw, *The Pharaoh*, pp. 119–20, has an account.

10. Aidan Dodson, *Amarna Sunset*, p. 111.

11. Aidan Dodson, *Amarna Sunset*, pp. 83–86.

Chapter 8

1. Arthur Weigall, letter to Francis Griffith, October 1, 1907. Quoted by T. G. H. James, *Howard Carter*, pp. 160–61.

2. T. G. H. James, *Howard Carter*, Chapters 6 and 7, cover Carter's role and the formation of the partnership with Lord Carnarvon.

3. Lord Carnarvon and Howard Carter, *Five Years Exploration at Thebes: A Record of Work Done 1907–1911* (London: Oxford University Press, 1912), pp. 1–2.

4. Many writers have dated the accident to 1901 or 1903, citing it as the reason Carnarvon repeatedly visited Egypt. In fact, the mishap seems to have occurred in August 1909, the date I use here. William Cross, *The Life and Secrets*, p. 77, discusses the issue and cites a report in *The Times* of September 15, 1909, to the effect that the Earl was recovering from an automobile accident. He attributes

the common error to the faulty memory of the Sixth Earl, who was a small child at the time. Lady Winifred Burghclere cites the earlier date in her memorial but may well be wrong, too, relying, as she likely did, on the Sixth Earl's childhood memory.

5. Described in T. G. H. James, *Howard Carter*, pp. 182ff.

6. The excavation is described in T. G. H. James, *Howard Carter*, pp. 187ff.

7. T. G. H. James reproduces the text of the agreement in Appendix II of *Howard Carter*.

8. Sir Alan Henderson Gardiner (1979–1963) made major contributions to Ancient Egyptian philology. His *Egyptian Grammar* (Oxford: Griffith Institute, reprint. ed. 1993) and *Egypt of the Pharaoh: An Introduction* (Oxford: Oxford University Press, 3rd ed., 1996) are classics. T. G. H. James, *Howard Carter*, Chapter 8, covers the events in this passage.

9. Described by William Cross, *The Life and Secrets*, pp. 87ff.

10. T. G. H. James, *Howard Carter*, Chapter 9, covers events in the remainder of this chapter.

11. Herbert Winlock, *Materials Used at the Embalming of King Tut-'Ank-Amun* (New York: Metropolitan Museum of Fine Art, 1941).

Chapter 9

1. Tutankhamun's death has provoked an avalanche of claims, studies, and theories, which invariably make newspaper headlines. We'll probably never know the precise cause of his demise. Rather than muddy the waters even further, I summarize the major theories very briefly here. See also Zahi Hawass et al., "Ancestry and Pathology in King Tutankhamun's Family," *Journal of the American Medical Association* 303, 7 (2010): 638–47.

2. Descriptions of the tomb are based on Nicholas Reeves, *The Complete Tutankhamun*, already cited.

3. Aidan Dodson, *Amarna Sunset*, p. 88; Charlotte Booth, *The Boy*, Chapter 6.

4. Description based on Garry J. Shaw, *The Pharaoh*, pp.180–88.

5. The Opening of the Mouth ceremony symbolically animated a mummy by opening its mouth so it could breath and speak in the afterlife. The ceremony was performed with a special ritual adze.

6. Aidan Dodson, *Amarna Sunset*, Chapter 5, analyzes this incident with his characteristic even-handedness. Quotes in this passage from p. 60 (Chapter 3) and p. 91. The Amarna Tablets are a gold mine of information on international diplomacy—if you can identify the players in the correspondence. The tablets bear often

opaque, sometimes insincere, messages about a diplomatic world where gifts and strategic royal marriages were the currency of stability. This makes the verification of the identity of the people referred to in the putative message from Ankhesena-mun a formidable challenge. The letter refers to the death of one "Nipkhururiya" and to "the king's wife." But was the writer Tutankhamun's widow? Most Egyptol-ogists believe that she was, because Nipkhururiya was her husband's prename, ap-parently transcribed accurately by a scribe into Akkadian. The alternatives such as Nefertiti or Merytaten writing on the death of Akhenaten seem far less credible given that there was an obvious successor. This is why I followed the scenario out-lined here. Everything between Tutankhamun's death and his funeral apparently dragged out over many months, far longer than the customary 70 days. The delay, caused by the Hittite king's suspicions, may well have galvanized opposition to a Hittite prince and led to the assassination of Zananzash.

7. Aidan Dodson, *Amarna Sunset*, p. 100.

8. Aidan Dodson, *Amarna Sunset*, p. 107.

9. Aidan Dodson, *Amarna Sunset*, pp. 111ff, describes these events, including quotes.

Chapter 10

1. Quoted by T. G. H. James, *Howard Carter*, p. 252.

2. The events of November 24 are best described by Carter himself: Howard Carter and A. C. Mace, *The Tomb of Tut.Ankh.Amen*, Chapters 5 and 6.

3. Howard Carter and A. C. Mace, *The Tomb*, p. 96. There is debate as to whether Carter actually said "It is wonderful," but who really cares!

4. I relied on Howard Carter and A. C. Mace, *The Tomb*, Chapter 6, for this passage.

5. T. G. H. Edwards, *Howard Carter*, pp. 259ff describes the surreptitious entry.

6. Letter from Lord Carnarvon to Alan Gardiner, December 17, 2012. Griffith Insti-tute Archives.

Chapter 11

1. Pierre Lacau (1873–1963) was a French Egyptologist, who served as Director of Antiquities in Egypt from 1914 to 1936. Subsequently, he was Professor of Egyp-tology at the Collège de France until 1947.

2. This passage draws on the analysis by T. G. H. Edwards, *Howard Carter*, pp. 264ff.

3. Albert Lythgoe (1868–1934) was founder of the Egyptology departments at both Boston's Museum of Fine Art and the Metropolitan Museum of Fine Art in New York. He spent ten years working in Egypt for the Met.

4. Arthur Cruttenden Mace (1874–1928) was a cousin of Flinders Petrie. He was an expert excavator and conservator of fragile artifacts as well as a fluent writer. Mace became Carter's right-hand man. His calm demeanor proved critical to the success of the tomb clearance.

5. *The Times* monopoly is a classic example of Carnarvon's narrow and privileged view of the world. Quoted from T. G. H. Edwards, *Howard Carter*, p. 278.

6. Quotes in this paragraph from T. G. H. Edwards, *Howard Carter*, p. 283.

7. Quotes in this paragraph from Howard Carter and A. C. Mace, *The Tomb*, p. 186.

8. T. G. H. Edwards, *Howard Carter*, pp. 289–90.

9. Letter from Mace to his wife, March 4, 1923. Quotes by T. G. H. Edwards, *Howard Carter*, p. 292.

10. Quoted in T. G. H. Edwards, *Howard Carter*, p. 293. Henry James Breasted (1865–1935) was an archaeologist and historian at the University of Chicago and founder of the university's celebrated Oriental Institute.

11. Quoted by Winifred Burghclere, "Biographical Sketch," p. 39.

12. Again, I rely on T. G. H. Edward's admirable analysis and description. *Howard Carter*, Chapters 12 to 15, tell the story for this passage.

13. Howard Carter, *Tut.Ankh.Amen: The Politics of Discovery* (London: Libri Publications, 1998) lays out Carter's statement in full.

14. Quoted from T. G. H. James, *Howard Carter*, p. 463.

Chapter 12

1. Giovanni Battista Belzoni, *Narrative of the Operations, and Recent Discoveries within the Pyramids, Temples, Tombs, and Excavations in Egypt and Nubia* (London: John Murray, 1820), pp. 156–57.

2. William Strunk, *The Elements of Style*. (New York: Grammar Inc., 2013), p. 1x.

3. Howard Carter and A. C. Mace, *The Tomb*, p. 97.

Index

Page numbers in *italics* indicate figures.

About the Author

Brian Fagan is Emeritus Professor of Anthropology at the University of California, Santa Barbara. Educated at Cambridge University, he spent his early career working on early farming villages in Africa. He is now regarded as one of the world's leading archaeological writers. His many books include a classic, *The Rape of the Nile*, as well as *The Little Ice Age* and *The New York Times* bestseller, *The Great Warming*. His most recent book is *The Intimate Bond: How Animals Shaped Human History*.